BUTTERFLY LOVE

Copyright © 2025 by Ken and Tabatha Claytor

All rights reserved. No part of this book may be reproduced or used in any manner without the written permission of the copyright owner except for the use of quotations in a book review. For more information, address: info@kenandtabatha.com

Unless otherwise noted, all Scripture quotations are taken from the Holy Bible, New International Version®, NIV®. Copyright ©1973, 1978, 1984, 2011 by Biblica, Inc.™ Used by permission. All rights reserved worldwide.
Cover Design by Valenda Martin
Edited by Art Fogartie
Published by Alive Church, Inc.

Printed in the United States of America
ISBN 979-8-9921266-1-7 (hardback)
www.KenandTabatha.com

BUTTERFLY LOVE
*a modern-day
love story*

Ken & Tabatha Claytor

For every heart that still longs for the butterflies. To the couple holding on by a thread. To the one who wonders if the spark can ever come back. To the one who believes love can be better than it's ever been—this book is for you. Wherever you are in your relationship, know this: there is always a way forward. And sometimes, the butterflies come back stronger than ever.

CONTENTS

INTRODUCTION

PART ONE: THE SPARK THAT STARTED IT ALL
- *one*   Shoot that Shot   05
- *two*   I Think I Can Fly   17
- *three*   The Break-Up   37

PART TWO: THE STORMS WE DIDN'T SEE COMING
- *four*   Is She Pregnant?   57
- *five*   The Honeymoon is Over   77
- *six*   Bye-Bye Butterflies   93
- *seven*   Divine Turnarounds   109

PART THREE: A LOVE THAT ENDURES
- *eight*   The Call   127
- *nine*   Miracles in the Mess   159
- *ten*   Turning it Around   193

APPENDIX

a note from us
INTRODUCTION

This isn't just a story about how we almost divorced. It's the story of what God did next. We've walked through brokenness, disappointment, healing, and restoration. We've experienced the beauty of falling in love—and the heartbreak of growing apart. But more than anything, we've seen the power of God to redeem what seemed lost and breathe life into what felt dead.

Butterfly Love is more than a feeling. It's a journey. And this book is the roadmap we wish we had—one filled with real moments, honest lessons, and hope for whatever season you're in. We don't have a perfect marriage. But we have a restored one. And if He did it for us, He can do it for you.

Whether you're dating, engaged, newly married, or decades in—this story is for you. It's a story of two imperfect people learning to love each other through every season, guided by a perfect God.

We're so glad you picked up this book. Let's go find the butterflies—together. ♡

part one
THE SPARK THAT STARTED IT ALL

one
SHOOT THAT SHOT

January 14th, 1998—cold, quiet, and completely forgettable, until she walked in. Wednesday nights in our college town had a predictable rhythm: hip-hop night at The Stone Pony, quarter pitchers at Speedys, and ladies' night at Elements—the biggest nightclub in the city and, conveniently, just 100 steps from my back door. I could've stayed in with a book, and part of me wanted to. I'm an introvert by nature—quiet, observant, and comfortable alone. But I've also always had just enough extrovert in me to enjoy a good party. That night, none of my boys wanted to go out, but I didn't need a crew. I threw on a jacket and went solo.

The club was unusually empty—maybe it was the freezing weather or the fact that classes had just started back up—but I didn't mind. I climbed up on the edge of the stage and sat, casually watching the handful of people on the dance floor. And that's when I saw her. Over near the bar. Tabatha. I'd seen her around campus since my freshman year, always thought she was the prettiest girl at West Virginia University, but I'd never had the right moment to approach her.

Until now.

I had tried once before—back during the first week of freshman year. At WVU, football ruled the fall, and like most students, I was at the stadium for one of those early-season games while the weather was still warm. I remember glancing over my shoulder and seeing her—Tabatha. Even then, something about her stood out. I thought, "Who is that?" I had to find out.

So, I did what any overly confident 18-year-old would do: I followed her. From a distance, of course. All the way from the stadium to the Mountain Lair—the student union where everybody went to eat and hang out. That meant hopping on the PRT, our elevated monorail system, and perfectly timing my arrival so I could accidentally bump into her.

Like a smooth criminal or a low-budget spy with a plan, I positioned myself near the back exit. I was ready—

just a casual approach, quick intro, ask her name, charm her a little. Easy. She walked out, and I stepped into her path like I'd rehearsed it: "Hey, how are you? What's your name?

Without missing a beat, she threw her hand up in my face, flashed an engagement ring, said "I'm engaged," and kept it moving. Well. I shot my shot. Welcome to college, baby

I remember that day. I was watching the football game with my girlfriends when they started teasing me saying, "Oooh! Watch out, Tab. Someone has their eye on you." He was sitting behind us, slightly to the right. I took a peek back and there he was. This handsome guy that none of us had ever seen. There was a mystery that surrounded him. We speculated that he had to be a transfer student or perhaps a grad student because no one else would have the confidence to go to a football game alone. This guy was different, and my friends and I were impressed. But regardless of how impressive he was, I was already taken. So, when he approached me, I didn't give him the time of day. I flashed him the ring and kept on walking.

So, technically, that night at Elements wasn't our first encounter. It was just the first time she actually noticed me. A year and a half had passed since that football game, and in that time, I watched her from a distance—go
through a breakup, pledge a sorority, disappear for a season, and then reappear like she never missed a beat.

Truth is, I needed that year and a half to grow up. If she had caught me a year earlier—bumping and grinding on the dance floor—she wouldn't have given me the time of day. And honestly, she would've been right.

But now? Now I was ready. I looked around the club that night and thought, "This is it. Tonight's my night." I was about to shoot my shot... again.

We had a saying in basketball: shooters keep shooting. I knew she wouldn't remember me from that awkward Mountain Lair moment. And that was a good thing. She struck me as the kind of woman who, once she was in a relationship, didn't even see other guys—which I respected. But now? The playing field was clear. I'd kept my distance, stayed out of the way, lurking—well, let's call it patiently waiting.

Tonight, I was stepping up. Fresh slate. New game. And I wasn't about to miss.

It was a cold, wintry night—and my twenty-second birthday—but I didn't feel like celebrating. I just wanted to stay home in my warm bed, far away from the party scene. But my girlfriends dragged me out of the house, not knowing I was feeling overwhelmed with life. I was no longer engaged, but the residue of a toxic relationship still had me vexed. On top of that, a couple of recent crushes had ended in heartbreak and left me thinking all men were dogs.

It was the old catch-22: I wanted to be in a relationship, but I was angry, annoyed, and irritated with the entire male population. I had a salty taste in my mouth—and a mindset to match: I can do bad all by myself.

Tabatha was in a sorority when we first met, which meant she was always surrounded by at least six to ten other ladies, what seemed like ten or so frat brothers and football players, plus a bunch of other guys just drooling—I mean hanging out—with them. It was virtually impossible to get through all those defensive linemen to even say hello.

But tonight was different. It was just her and two other friends. The crowd was thin—no football players, no frat brothers. It was go time.

I didn't think much about what I was going to say. That's never really been my thing. I figured I'd just let it happen naturally. But looking back, it might've been the best pickup line I've ever used. Ladies and gentlemen, this is why we've been married for over 25 years. I walked up behind her, on a Wednesday night, in a nightclub, and said, "Hi, what's your name?"

I already knew her name… but it was time for a fresh start.

She didn't even turn around

So, I said—wait for it—"I saw you in church on Sunday."

Now before you judge me, please understand: at that point in my life, I was what I call a Christian Atheist. That's someone who believes in God but lives like He doesn't exist. If you put me in a lineup with ten of my closest unsaved friends, you couldn't tell the difference. I drank like they drank, partied like they partied, slept around like they slept around. That's not a shot at them—it's just the truth about where I was.

I believed in God, went to church occasionally, and owned a Bible I never read. I believed, but I didn't live it. Just like so many people today, I was immature and carnal. Honestly, I didn't know any better.

So yes, there I was—in a nightclub—asking her about church.

And here's the thing: it wasn't meant to be a pickup line. I meant it with all my heart.

There was a little African Methodist Episcopal church on campus that I would go to sometimes. Not because I was A.M.E., but because it was the closest church to my apartment and, every now and then, they had fried chicken and cake after service. God bless that church, but to tell you the truth—I don't remember a single sermon ever preached there. Maybe it was great and my heart just wasn't in the space to receive it. But that's where I was.

So, if I wasn't too hung over or didn't have anything else to do on a Sunday, I'd slide in late, sit in the back, and leave early. That's how we Christian atheists roll. Church wasn't something I lived out—it was just something I checked off the list to feel like I'd done one good thing that week.

A few times, I saw Tabatha there. She never saw me—probably because I came in late and left early.

So when I said, "I saw you in church this Sunday," I was telling the truth.

And as soon as those words came out of my mouth, she turned around, smiled at me, and looked at me for the first time in a year and a half.

Winner.

My friends and I made our requests at the DJ booth and danced to all of our favorite songs. I went to the bar to get another drink when I noticed someone come from behind me. Immediately I was repelled. The last thing I wanted to do was be bothered by some guy while I was out with my girls just trying to have a good time. He sat down next to me and asked me for my name. Even though I was highly annoyed, I didn't want to be rude. At the same time, I wanted to send the message that I'm not interested.

So, I gave him the "blow off" response. While looking in the opposite direction I nonchalantly said, "Tabatha." I assumed this was going to go down like all of the other unsolicited pickup attempts. I would play nice, appease him with a fake number, and he would leave me alone the rest of the night. I know, that's so rude, but I had yet to discover the power of a good stern NO. But Ken's response caught me by surprise. He said, "I see you in church on Sundays." Now, up to this point I had not even looked at the man. My view of him was all peripheral. (Yes, I was giving him the side eye.) I had no idea what he looked like.

When he said "church," I turned my head so fast, I could have gotten whip lash. I responded, "How come I don't see you?" He said, "I come in late and sit in the back, so you don't see me, but I see you." He could have said he was Michael Jordan, a millionaire, or a prince and none of those would have piqued my interest in him. I'm convinced this was the only response that would have intrigued me.

At the time, I was searching for God. I wasn't saved. I didn't grow up in church and wasn't even sure if God was real. But I needed help. I was struggling with depression. I had a troubled family life. I lost my dad at an early age. I grew up with domestic violence, alcoholism, and abuse. I was sad a lot of the time and just completely lost. I thought, if God is real, I need to find Him. I bought a Bible and started to read it. I started to go to a church on campus. I tried to get my friends to go, but they weren't interested. So, when a stranger came up and shared the same desire to know God, it moved me.

I was so moved in fact, that I engaged in a full-blown conversation! At this point, he had all of my attention. I began to take mental notes. He was well-dressed, confident, and articulate. Usually, the kind of guys who approached me were more into themselves than me. They'd call me baby when I just gave them my name. They had zero communication skills, which was the biggest turnoff, or they'd steadily look down at my breasts instead of into my eyes. I'm sure I had a lot of cleavage showing, lol, but that's beside the point. It's so disrespectful! But so far, this guy Ken was shooting threes from down court and not missing. I got so caught up in the conversation, I didn't even realize how handsome he was. By the time I noticed his deep voice, dreamy hazel eyes, curly hair, and perfect smile, I'll admit, he had me a little flustered.

By the end of the conversation, he had won me over. He left the club that night with my real number. He likes to say that he was God's birthday gift to me. Well, I won't argue with him about that. He remains the best birthday gift I've received. No one can do it like God.

Looking back, this was the work of the Lord. It's amazing how our God is so filled with grace and mercy. He will reach us wherever we are, even when we don't really know Him ourselves. Now I get to say that our entire relationship has been built around church, even from night one…lol. Just not in the way that folks might think.

After we talked for a bit, I learned the reason Tabatha was out on a Wednesday night. It was her 22nd birthday and her friends dragged her out of the house and made her come out to celebrate on "ladies' night." So, there you have it. I was officially God's birthday gift to Tabatha. It does matter what you pray for right? And just think, she asked God for this before she was even saved. That will blow your theological mind.

What I didn't know at the time was that she was going to be the greatest gift that God ever gave me outside of Jesus. The Bible says it this way. "He who finds a wife finds a good thing, and obtains favor from the Lord," Proverbs 18:22. Unfortunately, it took me years to know how to care for my gift, cherish my gift, and love my gift. As you will see, I almost lost this gift, and returned it back to the sender a few times. But I am so glad I didn't.

There are three stages in a relationship: the infatuation stage, the fight for control stage, and the mature love stage. The infatuation stage is where we experience "butterfly love," the love that carries us away into blissful ignorance where we believe our spouse is perfect, their quirks are cute, and they can do no wrong. You get married thinking it will be like this forever, but this is not real love, it's infatuation. Endorphins are high and happy hormones are being released. But what happens when those endorphins disappear? You enter into the fight for power stage where many marriages end. Whereas before, your spouse could do no wrong, now they can do no right. That's where we were headed, right into the fight for power stage. This is where we almost lost it all. Hold on. It's about to get a little bumpy.

two

I THINK I CAN FLY

After that night at Elements, I decided I was going to do something different. Normally, when you meet someone new, you play it cool. You act like you've got so much going on, and maybe—if you have time—you'll give them a call. I'd tried that before, but it never really worked for me.

This time? I wasn't about to play games. I was calling Tabatha the very next morning.

I waited until about 11:00 a.m. I didn't want to seem like a weirdo stalker creep. But I also didn't want to wait too long and miss my shot. I picked up the phone, dialed her number, and when someone picked up, I said, "Hello, can I speak with Tabatha, please?"

I was still sleeping when Ken called. My roommate busted into my room yelling, "Tabby... Tabby! Ken is on the phone for you!" in her most fake professional voice, followed by giggling and obnoxious noises. I was caught off guard—who calls the very next morning? Before noon? Before I'm even out of bed?

But I was also a little... excited. I grabbed the phone, still groggy, but his voice woke me right up. Confident and calm. He asked me out to dinner—a real dinner. Not, your typical college guy "Can I come over to your place?" but an actual date at an actual restaurant. I was impressed. Who was this guy?

We had a great conversation that morning, and I decided to shoot my shot for real this time. I asked her out to dinner the next night. Now, this was a big move—because let's be honest, I still didn't know if she actually liked me, or if she gave me her number just to be nice and brush me off.

But when I asked, she said yes.

Man, you would've thought I'd just won the Super Bowl. I was pumped. The most beautiful girl on campus—the one everybody wanted to be with—said yes to going out with me.

I was walking around like, "Yeah. I'm the man."

Falling in Love

Our first date was Friday, January 16, 1998. I remember every detail like it was yesterday. I picked her up from her house and took her to dinner at the Boston Beanery in Morgantown, West Virginia. But before I pulled up, I made sure my ride was looking *pristine*.

Now, let me tell you about my car: a 1990 burgundy Toyota Camry. Yeah, it had about 190,000 miles on it, but don't get it twisted—it looked good. Come on, somebody! I bought it for $4,500 and was paying $145 a month on it like clockwork. It had leather seats, a moonroof, and those automatic seatbelts that slid into place when you closed the door. Back then, that was next level.

I even had the windows tinted with the darkest limo tint I could find. Was it legal? Absolutely not. Did I care? Absolutely not. I was 19 years old, rolling in my "Mack Mobile," and living my best life.

So, I pulled up to her house with Big Red chewing gum in my mouth and that "new car smell" air freshener tucked behind the seats. My car was shining like it had just rolled off the showroom floor, and I was feeling *ready*.

We drove over to the Boston Beanery, making small talk along the way. But honestly, my head was spinning. I kept thinking, This can't be real. I'm with the woman of my dreams.

When we sat down for dinner, the conversation flowed naturally. That's one of the things I loved most about Tabatha from the very beginning—she never tried to be someone she wasn't. She was kind, thoughtful, and her smile could light up the whole room.

Now, I was used to women who wanted me to act like a thug or treat them badly just to get their attention. I'd tried that before, but honestly, that just wasn't me. I grew up watching my dad love my mom and, when she passed, they'd been married for nearly 50 years. That's the kind of love I wanted. Sure, I tried to play the role of a wannabe player, but deep down, I was always a hopeless romantic.

Our first date was amazing. The chemistry was easy, the conversation was enlightening, and we clicked in a way that felt effortless. Now, this was a long time ago, so I don't remember every detail of what we talked about, but I'll never forget one part of the conversation. Somehow, we started talking about profanity.

Out of nowhere, we discovered that neither of us cussed. Like, ever. That was huge for me because I'd never met anyone like that before. Growing up, someone once told me that people who use a lot of profanity might do so because they don't have the vocabulary to express themselves properly. That stuck with me, so I just never went there. Sure, I'd say stuff like "freaking" or "what the blank" (corny, I know), but actual cussing? Nah, it wasn't my thing.

Finding out that Tabatha was the same way felt like one of those little God winks—like He was saying, Yep, this is the one.

I was a little nervous when Ken came to pick me up. After some of my past experiences with guys, I was hesitant—very hesitant—to let myself like another guy. I didn't know much about him yet, but Ken was already making me throw my hesitations out the window.

He seemed so much older than me. He drove his own car, paid for my meal, and even asked if we could see each other again. Everything about him just felt different.

But on the way home, I was super nervous. I knew he was going to kiss me—I could feel it coming—and honestly, I wanted him to kiss me, but I was so scared. What if he messes it up with an aggressive kiss goodbye? What if he tries to rip my clothes off on the first date? I had all these thoughts running through my mind. Is he really into me, or am I just another trophy for his collection? Please, let him be a gentleman.

His car was spotless, sparkling clean inside and out. It was warm and toasty, and it smelled amazing—like leather and vanilla, masculine but sweet. The music was perfect, not so loud that we had to raise our voices, but loud enough to enjoy the lyrics and still have a great conversation.

When we pulled up to my house, he put the car in park, and I could feel my heart pounding. I wanted to melt into my seat. This is it. Our first kiss. Please, let it be good.

He leaned over and kissed me. It was perfect. Long enough to say, I really like you, but short enough to say, I respect you. I was too nervous to completely enjoy it in the moment, but I definitely felt it. That kiss sealed the deal for me.

Ken was different. "I think I really like him."

It didn't take us long to fall in love, but I felt like our romance needed a little push from me. Shortly after our first date, I found out that Tabatha worked the overnight shift at Stalnaker Hall. For those who don't know, Stalnaker was a dorm for upperclassmen, and Tabatha worked the front desk during the graveyard shift.

Now, I happened to know her supervisor, Raphael. He was an international student from Africa, and he was in charge of staffing for multiple dorms. So, I called him up and said, "Hey bro, I need a job." He asked me where I wanted to work, and I said, "Stalnaker Hall, and I'm willing to work the overnight shift." He paused for a second and said, "You know, I just hired a young lady named Tabatha to work there too."

"Oh really?" I said, acting like I had no idea. "Well, that's perfect. Put me on the same shift with her."

Now, I'll admit—years later, I can see how that might have been borderline stalking. But hey, the proof is in the pudding. I walked into work that first night, and there she was, sitting at the front desk. She looked at me and said, "What are you doing here?"

I grinned and said, "I'm reporting to work. What are *you* doing here?" Acting like I didn't know the whole thing was a setup.

And just like that, we were working the midnight to 6:00 am shift together. Alone.

Ken was such a bad influence on me when it came to working at Stalnaker Hall! Before he showed up, I was doing great. The job was simple: watch the front door. I worked the night shift—usually from around 12:00 am to 6:00 am. I'd do my homework, get some studying in, and if things were quiet, I'd put my head down on the desk and catch a quick nap.

Then Ken came along and completely wrecked my routine.

From day one, everything was a party to him. He was loud, broke every rule in the book, and made it nearly impossible for me to stay focused. The very first night, he found a piano in one of the rooms and started playing and singing—loudly—at midnight!

He'd walk up and down the halls talking to people like he was hosting some late-night social hour. And if that wasn't enough, he often convinced me to leave my shift early. He made me so nervous. "This man is going to get me fired!"

But as much as he drove me crazy... I couldn't stop laughing. He made everything fun. And honestly? I liked it.

After that, we were pretty much inseparable. From the outside, Tabatha seemed like this super popular sorority girl that no one could touch. She had this vibe, like she was on a whole other level. But when I got to know her, I realized she wasn't even aware of how other people saw her.

She was the kindest, warmest, most thoughtful, fun-loving person I had ever met. She wasn't like any of the other girls I had dated before. She didn't want a thug or someone who played games. She wanted kindness, respect, and honesty—straight up. She had this openness to God and spiritual things, even though she didn't know God for herself yet.

A few weeks went by, and I was really liking me some Ken Claytor. We were constantly talking and learning more about each other. But somehow, we still hadn't talked about our ages. Ken had this way of dancing around the topic, and I didn't push—until one day.

We were at his place, and he was sitting at his desk working on something. I noticed his class ring on the desk and picked it up. It had 1996 engraved on it. My brain immediately went into calculation mode. Okay, I graduated in 1994... I'm 22. He graduated in 1996... he's 20.

At first, I felt a little pang of disappointment. I thought he was older. But that disappointment was just a pebble compared to the boulder that came next. I asked, "Ken, are you 20?"

Without missing a beat, he said, "I'm 19."

NINETEEN. I froze. My mind started spiraling. He's only 19?! I'm 22! I'm dating a teenager! I'm robbing the cradle! I'm a cougar! Ken, of course, picked up on my internal meltdown. He stopped what he was doing, locked eyes with me like I was the only person in the world, and turned on the charm. His eyes lit up, and he gave me that smile that always made me melt. Then, in his smoothest, most movie-star tone, he said, "Girl, age ain't nothin' but a number."

I couldn't even argue with him. He grabbed my hand and added, "Your birthday is in January. Mine is in May. It's barely over two years. No big deal." I melted. He could've told me the sky was green, and I would've believed him in that moment. Later that day, I told my roommates, and they laughed so hard they couldn't breathe. They teased me mercilessly, but they liked him too. We were all under his spell.

So yes—my name is Tabatha, and I'm a cougar and a cradle robber.

When she says we were constantly talking and learning about each other, she means it. We were inseparable. I know we drove our friends crazy. We were together *all the time* and didn't do much without each other. I can still remember showing up at her house and walking right through six or eight frat brothers who were posted up on the front porch. They'd give me these looks like they couldn't stand me, but they couldn't do a thing about it.

Why? Because Tabatha would come running out, give me the biggest hug, and kiss me right in front of everyone. No games. Not once. Ever. She liked me and wasn't afraid to let the whole world know.

Her house was always packed with people. Back then, you didn't really see couples being openly affectionate. Sure, there were hookups or people who liked each other but they kept it on the down low. But Tabatha? She didn't care. She'd grab my hand, sit on my lap, and basically announce to everyone, *This is my man.*

I loved that about her. If she hadn't taken that stance, I probably would've gotten beat up—no lie. I'm only 5'9" and walking past all those "brothers" who were trying to protect her took a whole lot of confidence. But she made it easy for me. Without her, it wouldn't have worked.

That was the thing I loved most about Ken—then and now—his confidence. He wasn't a people pleaser. In college, when everyone seemed obsessed with impressing others, Ken just did his own thing. He wasn't trying to fit in or be part of the cool crowd. He wasn't trying to be cool—he just was.

One time, he invited me to his apartment for what he called a "little party." He said, "I'm having a party at my house. You should come." I figured it would be a chill vibe with a handful of people. So, I gathered a couple of girlfriends and showed up. What we walked into was absolute chaos.

We could barely get through the door. The place was packed. There were drunk people passed out on the floor, and we had to step over bodies just to get through the living room. Then there were people inhaling nitrous oxide from balloons (and I'm pretty sure that was illegal). My friends and I looked at each other like, What kind of party is this?!

We made our way to the kitchen and spotted Ken standing by the back door which was connected to the fire escape. He was holding a huge wad of cash, charging people an entry fee, and there was a line of people wrapped all the way down the fire escape trying to get in.

I thought, "Where are these people even going to fit? We're already packed in here like sardines!" A little while later, Ken grabbed the microphone and started rapping. The crowd loved it. He had the whole place hyped.

In that moment, I couldn't decide whether to laugh, roll my eyes, or walk out. But one thing was clear: Ken was doing his own thing, and somehow, it was working.

We did everything together—movies, bowling, ice skating, studying, working. Tabatha was my partner in everything.

She was also fun for me because she was so naive to the world. On the outside, she seemed like this sophisticated girl with money, friends, and popularity. I thought she was raised with a silver spoon in her mouth.

I couldn't have been more wrong.

I had no clue about her upbringing or even her background. That's why you should never judge a book by its cover. The cover of her life read: I'm pretty, I'm popular, I'm well to do, and I know who I am. The book of her life read much differently, as I would soon find out.

But that was an adventure for me. I was attracted to her lack of world exposure. It triggered something in me that I really enjoyed. I don't know if it was the pastor part of me that I didn't even realize was there, or if I simply wanted to rescue the damsel in distress. Whatever it was, I loved helping her discover new things.

Tabatha had never been on a plane, never been to the beach, never been skiing, and didn't really know how to swim. Shoot, she didn't even have a driver's license.

I got to teach her how to drive. I'll never forget her jumping in my "Mack Mobile"—my 1990 Toyota Camry—and practicing in parking lots as I gave her instructions. I can tell by the way she drives these days that I didn't do that great of a job, but it was fun while it lasted, lol.

My driving? Don't get me started on his! But let me not get distracted. Ken didn't make it hard to figure out how he felt about me. If he saw me in public, he'd greet me with a kiss on the cheek and hold my hand. He treated me like a lady, whether we were alone or in front of a crowd.

The better I got to know him, the more I loved him. We were so different yet so much alike. I was a first-generation college student, born and raised in the projects of a very small town. In many ways, I was experiencing life for the first time. Ken came along and became the wind beneath my wings. He showed me more, supported my dreams, and made me better.

One of my favorite memories was when I decided to take her to an event called Bridge Day. It's a big deal in West Virginia, held every year at the New River Gorge Bridge, which at the time was the tallest arch bridge in America. Thousands of people come from all over to parachute off the bridge or raft in the river below.

I asked her one day, "Sweetheart, have you ever heard of Bridge Day?" Of course, she hadn't. So, I said, "I'm taking you to Bridge Day."

We got in the car and drove a few hours to get there. She was halfway asleep most of the drive, but as we got close, I said, "Sweetheart, wake up—here comes the bridge!"

She sat up, full of excitement, and looked out the window. We crossed this tiny little bridge, the kind you'd see on a normal interstate, and I said, "There it is!"

She looked at it, confused and disappointed, and said, "That's it? What's the big deal?"

I couldn't hold it in. I busted out laughing and said, "That's not the bridge! We're still a few minutes away."

I know it was wrong to mess with her like that, but her innocence and trust made moments like that so much fun. Decades later, we still laugh about it.

We still laugh? Maybe he still laughs. I remember that bridge incident. He thought it was hilarious, but let me tell you—I did not find it funny. I didn't want to hurt his feelings so I was genuinely trying to be polite; looking at that tiny little bridge and trying to find something positive to say. How was I supposed to know he was lying?

Of course, it wasn't all one-sided. Tabatha brought out things in me, too. For example, she proofread all my papers and edited my assignments in college. Grammar and spelling have never been my strong suits.

She also made sure I was fed and taken care of. I wasn't a great cook so she would fix me breakfast. She was a vegetarian, but she would fix me French toast, eggs and bacon. Being a college student, I would eat fast food, or just whip something together to survive, but she was a great cook. They say the way to a man's heart is through his stomach. I am a living witness to that. She could make anything from scratch. I thought, not only does my girlfriend

I THINK I CAN FLY

look like a bi-racial Miss America, but she is also doggone Betty Crocker. I am "the man!"

Seriously, some of my favorite dates with Tabatha were the ones where she'd make us a picnic. She'd pack a basket with all my favorite foods, organized in a way that only she could. We'd go to a park, lay down a blanket, and spend hours just eating, talking, and laughing. To this day, I don't think there's ever been a more hopelessly romantic couple in college history.

Ken loves food, and I figured that out pretty quickly. One day, I stopped by his apartment while he was in the middle of cooking himself a meal. I thought it was adorable. He made chicken and green beans. To tell you the truth—it was a pitiful-looking chicken and green beans. But I was impressed that he cared enough to cook himself a real meal. Most college students were living off fast food, but there Ken was, trying to cook like a grown up.

That's when I decided I'd make a meal for him. The first thing I cooked for him was a vegetarian breakfast—scrambled eggs, French toast, and breakfast potatoes. Later, he confessed that he didn't think my vegetarian meal was going to be good. But he loved it. And ever since that day, I've been cooking for him.

Even now, he'll make something like a sandwich, and it'll be okay. But when I make the same sandwich, he says it's phenomenal. I just smile and say, "Baby, you've always needed me to bring some flavor into your life."

Listen, we weren't just falling in love; we were building something special. Tabatha had a complicated family situation, so holidays were tough for her. Easter was coming up, and when I found out she wasn't planning to go home, I didn't hesitate. I invited her to come home with me and spend Easter with my family.

At first, she wasn't sure. I get it—meeting the family is a big step and she didn't want to intrude. But I assured her it wouldn't be a problem, and eventually, she agreed.

We drove to my hometown, Beckley, West Virginia, where she met my parents and sister. I showed her the house I grew up in and the high school where I played basketball. Seeing her in my world, with the people who mattered most to me, just solidified what I already knew—this girl was special.

By the end of that trip, I knew Tabatha wasn't just my girlfriend. She was my partner.

That trip to Beckley won me over completely. Meeting Ken's family, seeing the home where he grew up, and getting a glimpse into his world made me realize just how special he was. He didn't just invite me into his life; he made me feel like I belonged there.

Butterflies Everywhere

I knew it was happening when we started having a hard time getting off the phone. The first couple months of our relationship were nearly perfect. I honestly can't remember one disagreement or argument. It felt like two long-lost friends had finally found each other.

There were nights we'd talk on the phone for hours, neither of us wanting to hang up. It got so bad one night, I think she actually dozed off while we were talking. And when she woke up, we *still* didn't want to hang up. I remember saying, "You hang up." She'd say, "No, you hang up." Then I'd say, "You hang up." And neither of us would do it. We were drunk in love—years before Beyoncé put a song to it.

A couple of months into the relationship, it was obvious we were boyfriend and girlfriend. Everybody knew it. We drove people crazy with it. But even though it was clear how we felt about each other, we still hadn't said those three magical words: *I love you.*

Being in love with Ken was like being on some kind of happy pill. We were obsessed with each other. I loved him, and I knew he loved me. But I wasn't the kind of girl to say "I love you" first. I didn't want to say it and then have him feel obligated to say it back. I wanted it to come from him, to mean something real.

Ken was bold and confident—sure of himself in a way I admired. I knew that if he said it, he would mean it. So, I waited.

It was late—had to be around 3:00 am. I know that because we were sitting on the front balcony of my apartment on High Street.

Let me explain High Street for a second. It was the main strip in our little college town where all the bars, clubs, and restaurants were. And no, it wasn't called High Street because everyone walking down it was high—although, let's be real, some of them probably were.

Anyway, it was late. The street was quiet. No cars, no people, no noise. Just us. Tabatha was sitting on my lap, her head resting on my shoulder. We were just holding each other, and it felt like the rest of the world didn't exist.

The feeling I had that night was like nothing I'd ever felt before. I'd told girls I loved them before, but looking back, I don't even know if I liked them compared to how I felt about Tabatha. This was different.

I felt "butterflies" in my stomach. The feeling was so strong, it was like if I wasn't holding her in my arms, I might have floated away.

So, there we were, sitting on my balcony on High Street in the middle of the night. And before I could second-guess myself, I said, "Tabatha… I love you."

Whoa! Did I just say that? Yes, I did. And what did she do? Honestly, I don't even remember. I think I fainted. Tabatha, help me out here!

That night was magical. Our emotions were skyrocketing—joy was a ten, happiness was a ten, love was a ten. Our connection was off the charts.

When I think about that moment, sitting on his lap on the balcony, with the stars above us and the world so still, it felt like we were the only two people alive. It's a memory I carry with me, frozen in time, like a snow globe. When I think about it, I picture us in that snow globe, sitting on the balcony, and when you shake it, little stars swirl all around.

Words can't describe the feeling of that night when we told each other we were in love for the first time. But I do remember the butterflies.

Ken literally said, "My stomach feels like it's jumping." And I said, "Mine too, like butterflies."

There you have it. "I'm in love, round and round we go, out of control, I'm in love." I was in love with the woman of my dreams, and she loved me too. The air felt different up there. The reds were redder, the blues were bluer. The whole world just looks better when you're in love.

I felt like I was flying. Unfortunately, this plane would be grounded far too soon…

three

THE BREAK-UP

The first six months were amazing. We were in what they call the infatuation stage—the season where the other person can do no wrong. Scientists say it can last anywhere from three months to three years. During that time, your body releases a rush of feel-good chemicals, and it creates what we like to call the butterfly effect.

And yes, the butterfly effect is real. That flutter you get in your stomach? It's not just your imagination. Your brain is flooding your system with so many endorphins that you become temporarily blind to the other person's flaws, quirks, and shortcomings (and trust me, we all have them).

Most people reach this stage and assume those feelings will last forever. But the truth is—that's not how love actually works.

There are three stages to relationships:

The Infatuation Stage

The Fight for Control Stage

The Mature Love Stage

Most people don't make it past the second stage. That's where breakups and divorces happen because people don't realize that these are just *natural* stages in any relationship. They start asking questions like:

Where did the love go?

What happened to the romance?

Who *are* you, and what did you do with the person I fell in love with?

Sometimes, that's a fair question. But a lot of the time, nothing really changed—you were just blinded in the beginning. The infatuation stage is real love, but it's *emotional* love. It's not mature love. It's not agape love. It's the *beginning* of love. It's what I like to call *butterfly love*.

And *butterfly love* can be a beautiful thing…until reality shows up.

I was in a butterfly garden—totally, fully, and completely smitten with Ken Claytor. I thought we were just having fun, laughing, going on dates, and making beautiful memories together. And we were.

What I didn't understand was that we were deep in the infatuation stage. That season where the flaws fade into the background—and trust me, we both had plenty. But this stage didn't just cause me to overlook his imperfections; it gave me an escape from my present worries. I was swept up in the "too good to be true" high of falling in love.

I was obsessed with how brilliant he was, how handsome, how kind. I bought him gifts, cooked him meals, studied his likes and dislikes. I went all in on Ken Claytor. And in the process, I forgot about my own pain—my struggles, my trauma, the sadness I'd buried for so long.

I had battled depression for years. But when Ken came into my life, it was like someone turned on a light. The panic attacks, the suicidal thoughts, the weight I'd been carrying—they all faded into the background.

For a season.

That's what butterfly love can do. It can make you feel like everything is finally okay. Until one day, you wake up and realize…the problems never actually left. You just found a temporary escape.

I had no idea Tabatha struggled with depression for ten years before we met. I also had no clue that, when we first started dating, she wasn't even enrolled in college. She held that bit of information back from me. She made it seem like she was going to class, but the truth was, she was just going to work and trying to find a way to get back into school. I thought all those dates and picnics we went on were just her making time for me. I had no idea she actually had the time—because she wasn't in school.

To my credit, I was the first person in my family to go to college. If I hadn't followed my then-fiancé to school, I probably wouldn't have made it out of the projects. I didn't apply anywhere else—I just went where he went. Getting out of the hood and into college was a miracle. Staying in, well, that was another story. With all the childhood trauma I carried, school was hard. I didn't have the emotional support or financial stability I needed. No parents, no family to help me figure out life. I was the classic case of "you can take the girl out of the hood, but you can't take the hood out of the girl." I was making leaps of progress as it related to where I came from. But it seemed like when I took two steps forward academically, I'd take three steps back, emotionally.

So, I did what we did where I was from. I drank, and I drank, and I drank.

Tabatha came up with this bright idea. She figured there was one surefire way to get back into school and have it paid for: Join the Army. She talked to me about it—about what it would mean for us. By that point, we had been together for about six months, and we both saw our future together. So, I signed up to be a military husband. The plan was for her to go into ROTC. They'd help pay for school, she'd graduate, become an officer, and wherever she got stationed, I'd just move with her. It wasn't my plan, and I didn't think it was the best idea, but I went with it. She believed it was her only option, so I supported her.

I enrolled in the ROTC program thinking, This is my chance to become strong. The Army promised to train me to be mentally tough, and I believed that if I could just toughen up, I could finally beat depression. So, I left for officer's training in June of 1998. Ken and I had been dating for about six months. We were completely in love, and this was the first time we had ever been apart.

But it was only six weeks. I figured I'd be back soon, and we'd pick up right where we left off.

Or so I thought…

Tabatha was stationed at Fort Knox, Kentucky. For six weeks, she was trained for war. What we didn't know was that the real battle wasn't just on the field—it was inside of her. Since this was before cell phones, communication wasn't easy. She didn't get a lot of calls, and when she did, it was hard to catch each other. I don't remember our talking much at all during those six weeks.

I was in Washington, D.C., living with a buddy of mine. I was sleeping on his couch, but I had an internship at Enterprise Rent-A-Car in Rockville, Maryland. I was making seven dollars an hour, and I thought I was rich. Life was good—I was in D.C., I had a steady girlfriend that I loved, and I had a job that paid better than anything I'd had before. Minimum wage was $4.25 per hour at this point. But man, I missed Tabatha. I was lovesick. I could barely function. I'd write her letters, telling her how much I missed her. She'd write back when she could.

I know it was only six weeks, but it felt like forever.

One day, I was sitting through an internship training in Charleston, West Virginia. I knew Tabatha was flying back from officer's training that same day. I was sitting in that class, not hearing a word they were saying. I couldn't take it.

I got up, walked out of the training, got in my car, and drove two hours to Morgantown, West Virginia, just to see her. I was pumped. I had gone and bought her a bouquet of flowers. I was going to knock on her door, surprise her, and everything would go back to normal. Big Red chewing gum in my mouth, dressed to impress, I pulled up to her apartment and knocked on the door.

She opened it. She was surprised. But not in an Oh my God, you're here! kind of way. More like an Oh…what are you doing here? kind of way. I gave her the flowers. We had an awkward hug. An awkward kiss. It was all just, awkward.

I'm glad you remember because I don't. Honestly, it all sounds like the end of a movie where everything has gone horribly wrong, and they start playing that slow, depressing music in the background. I don't remember what I said. I don't

THE BREAK-UP

remember how it happened. But somehow, you got the message: It's over. I just want to be friends.

My heart shattered into a million pieces. The butterflies? Gone. Replaced by a nauseous, gut-wrenching pain I had never felt before. If this was heartbreak, I never wanted to fall in love again. This was too much. I wasn't supposed to be that guy. I was the cool dude. The ladies' man. The Man. So why was I crying so much? Why did it feel like my whole world had collapsed?

I don't know how to explain it, but breaking up with Ken felt like I was watching myself do something I didn't want to do. He hadn't done anything wrong. He was good to me. He loved me. But I wasn't in a place where I could love him back the way he deserved. What he didn't know—what I couldn't explain—was that I was slipping. The depression had returned. The weight of everything I'd been running from was pressing down on me again.

And for some reason, being with Ken made it worse.

He made me feel worthy. He made me feel beautiful. But I felt damaged. I felt unworthy. I was self-sabotaging, and I knew it. I had just finished Army training. I had faced some of the toughest challenges and come out stronger. I had a boyfriend who genuinely loved me. But deep down, I didn't believe I deserved any of it. I didn't feel good enough—for him, for this relationship, for the life I wanted.

I went back to D.C. to finish out my summer internship. It was probably late July by this point, and school was starting in a few weeks. I was done. Completely wrecked. One of my best friends and roommate Mike tried to cheer me up. We went out, partied, drank—I tried to distract myself from the pain.

Didn't work.

I tried to be with other girls.

Worked a little.

Nah…not really.

Nothing could shake the feeling that I had lost *her*. And worse, I had no closure. How could something so good end like that?

This, my friends, was one of the worst seasons of my life. It felt like it lasted forever, even though it was only a few weeks. If you've ever been through a bad breakup or a divorce, I see you. I may not know the depths of your pain, but I know what it feels like to walk through the fire of heartbreak. And here's what I've learned: **Storms don't last forever.**

Rejection from a person can sometimes be God's protection. If someone is meant for you, God will turn their heart back to you. And if He doesn't? That means He has something better. A lot of times, rejection has nothing to do with you and everything to do with them. Even if they try to blame you for it. Even if they give you no real explanation.

Trust me. It's a cover-up.

August rolled around, and I was back at school. I decided it was time to man up. Tabatha might have been a top pick on campus, but I was no chump either. I told myself, "I can make it. I'll be fine. Let me get my cool back". And honestly? By the time school started, I was okay. Still sad. Still carrying the weight of it all. But I was moving forward. Still... I couldn't shake the feeling that I had lost more than just my love. I had lost my friend. So, I did something that, looking back, I'm pretty sure I did on purpose. I took a little drive. I just happened to drive down her street. You know, just in case I accidentally ran into her.

And sure enough, there she was. I saw her in the distance, walking home from work. Alone. I slowed down, rolled down my window—music on, tinted windows looking clean—and pulled up next to her like it was nothing. "Hey," I said, casually. "Long time no see." And to my surprise... She smiled. She wasn't awkward. She wasn't avoiding me. She was actually happy to see me.

I was happy to see him. I could tell from our conversation—something was still there. I was working at 7-Eleven and Ken started showing up. At first, I thought it was a coincidence. But then I noticed...he wasn't just stopping by. He was shopping. At 7-Eleven. Which, let's be honest, is not exactly the place you go for groceries. But every time he came in, we'd talk. And every time we talked, something old—

something familiar—sparked between us. So, we decided to meet up.

I could sense there were things she struggled with beneath the surface. But it wasn't until that conversation that I realized just how deep it ran. That's when I found out the truth. The real truth. Tabatha had been battling depression since she was twelve years old. She had been carrying a weight I didn't fully understand—a burden she had learned to mask, even from me.

I confessed! Like the woman with the issue of blood, I told it all. I was first diagnosed with depression when I was twelve. I had a troubled childhood. And I believe my family did the best they knew how, but life was hard for us. I was born and raised in the projects of a small town in Pennsylvania. My dad died when I was six, leaving my mom alone—and pregnant. After that, I lived next door with my grandma. She raised me like I was her own. Her house was my safe place, a shelter from the chaos—the drinking, the fighting, the things no child should ever have to see.

Before the age of ten, I had been molested, beaten, and exposed to things that stole my innocence before I even understood what innocence was. But no matter how bad things got, I always had Grandma's house. Until I didn't. She got sick. And within months, she was gone. I was twelve. And in my twelve-year-old mind, all I could think was: Who's going to protect me now? That's when I disengaged. I stopped talking. I

THE BREAK-UP

shut down. And that's when the doctor diagnosed me with depression.

I sat there, listening to her, trying to process it all. How had I not known? How had she hidden all of that from me?

After Grandma died, I was thrown into a home filled with domestic violence, alcoholism, and abuse. That's when I became a fighter. I decided that if no one else was going to take care of me—I'd do it myself. I was the one who called the cops when fights broke out. I was the one who called the ambulance when someone was bleeding. I was the one who locked the doors at night, put out cigarette butts so the house didn't catch fire, and made sure my siblings were safe in their beds.

I got engaged at sixteen years old. I didn't want to. I knew I was too young, and honestly, I was a little embarrassed. But I played it off like it was okay. The truth? It was an abusive relationship. Statistics say if you grow up witnessing domestic abuse, you'll likely end up in it—either as the aggressor or the victim. That was me. On the outside, I was all smiles, the good girl, the one who had it all together. But on the inside? I was controlled. Trapped.

I followed my fiancé to college. Not because I had dreams of higher education. Not because I had a plan for my future. I just followed him because, at that time, he was my only plan. I applied nowhere else. No one told me I could do anything different. But once I got to college, something in me woke up. I started seeing life outside of him. I started realizing I had choices. I didn't have to stay in that relationship. I didn't have to live my life under someone else's control.

So, I finally ended it. It was not easy. He didn't just let me go. He stalked me, threatened me, even assaulted me. One time, he completely ransacked my apartment. It took several failed attempts, and the help of a very dear friend, but I finally stood my ground. I walked away. For good. I thought that was the end of my struggle. But it wasn't. Even though I was free from him, I was still trapped in something even bigger. Depression.

The next step in my freedom should have been simple: break free from depression. But depression isn't like a toxic relationship. You can't just walk away from it. It follows you. Clings to you. Wears you like a second skin.

After I left my fiancé, I started drinking more. It numbed the pain. It helped me sleep my worries away. For a while, I had it "under control." I was drinking, but I was still going to class, still working. Then I went home for a visit, and I saw one of my family members with a black eye. Just like that, I spiraled. The panic attacks came back. The nightmares. The feeling that I wasn't safe.

At twenty-one, I walked into the student health center and sat down with a psychiatrist. After telling them everything, I was diagnosed with severe depression and anxiety disorder

THE BREAK-UP

and started taking antidepressants. And for a little while, it helped. Until it didn't.

I lived in cycles. Six months of being okay. Six months of barely holding on. I'd fight my way out of the pit, thinking, This time, I'm free. Then, somehow, I'd fall right back in. Then came Ken, and he changed everything. He pulled me out of the pit. He was like light in a place that had been dark for too long. He made me happy. He made me want to enjoy life. He was my reason to get up in the morning. But that was the problem. He wasn't supposed to be the one that made me happy; the one who fulfilled me. Only God could fill that void. Ken wasn't enough to satisfy the God-sized hole in my soul. Looking back, I can see it clearly now: I broke up with Ken searching for something that only God could give me.

Thinking back, I didn't understand any of this. In my mind, if she had been looking for God, why did she have to lose me to find Him? But that's where a lot of relationships go wrong. We place our spouse or our significant other on the seat of our heart where God belongs. Neither of us knew at the time, but she needed some space to heal and get that right.

And that's why I am not sorry that we broke up. I am sorry that Ken was so miserable. I hate that he experienced so much pain on my behalf, but I broke up with him because I was in the ugly cycle headed back down into the pit. When I met Ken, I was on a journey to find God. Remember, the pickup line? "I saw you in church." Well, I was not saved. I did not know God. I was searching for God but on my way to find him, I found Ken. I started to follow Ken. Ken made me happy. Ken made me feel loved. Ken brought joy to my life. When I met Ken, I took my eyes off God.

Like I said, breaking up with Ken was an act of self-sabotage. I was being influenced by spiritual darkness stronger than I had ever felt. There was a battle going on for my soul and neither Ken nor I knew it. When I returned home from Fort Knox, I became so depressed. I was being attacked with suicidal thoughts. I was mixing alcohol and antidepressants. I began to withdraw from life, including my relationship with Ken. He didn't know about the depression, and I didn't know how to tell him. So, it was easier to make up some flaky reason to break up.

Here's why I don't regret the breakup. When Ken was gone, my attention went back to God. It was like I got back on the road where I left off. I was alone in my apartment when I heard a knock at the door. It was a few ministers from a local church, and they told me about Jesus and invited me to church. I prayed with them and asked Jesus to be my Lord. I got born again. I finally found God! I changed in a moment. I felt love, true unconditional love for the first time. From that day, I never had another suicidal thought. The desire I had to drink uncontrollably left. I stopped partying. I started going to church. I got baptized and that was the beginning of my walk with God.

If I had not broken up with Ken, I would not have found the one true love of my life, Jesus Christ, King of the World. I hurt Ken when I broke up with him, but he didn't want that old Tabatha anyway. When he drove by me that day, he sensed a change. The change was a new Tabatha, a new creation. He was seeing God in me for the very first time.

A Change of Heart

It was on again—quickly. Yeah, we had only been broken up for two or three months, but take it from me—it felt like three or four years at the time. I should've been happy. I should've been all-in, ready to pick up where we left off. But this time, things were different. The butterflies weren't there like before. I was still bitter. I was angry that she had put me through all that drama. And deep down, I wanted her to earn my love and trust again. (Sign #1 of a problem relationship right there.)

I let my pride step in. I wanted to haze her a little. I wanted her to pay for what she did to me. We were together, but I wasn't as nice to her all the time. I'd bring up the breakup often, just to remind her.

I was still bitter, but at the same time, I didn't want to let her go. I loved this girl so much. I didn't want to live my life without her. After being back together for a few months, I thought, "I need to lock this up. She's the one. I want her to be my wife."

Did I mature out of my bitterness and anger? No. I just put it to the side for the time being. I just had this inner knowing that she would be my wife. Looking back, I think I had known it all along.

Freshman year—before we officially met, before she had any idea who I was—I was riding around with my friend Kabelo, an African exchange student I hung out with in college. We were talking about the women on campus, just throwing names out there, and I told him, "Tabatha will be my wife one day. Watch and see."

That was not a normal conversation for us. We were freshmen. Marriage wasn't even on our radar. Especially not marriage to someone who was engaged to somebody else at the time. But I said it. And I meant it.

Thinking back, that had to be the prophetic nudging of God. He has always had this funny way of showing me things before they happen. One night, I was out to dinner with the CFO of the nightclub, Elements. We weren't talking about anything deep—just life, business, random stuff. Then out of nowhere, I said, "Later on when I start preaching…"

I stopped. He stopped. We both just stared at each other. "What did you just say?" he asked.

I had no idea where it came from. I knew we weren't talking about God. We weren't talking about ministry. But somehow, those words just came out. We sat there for a moment in awkward silence, then moved on to something else. But I never forgot it.

I say all of that to say—God knows our future way before we do. He formed us in our mother's womb and set a plan in motion before we even knew how to say yes to Him. If we're paying attention, He speaks to us about our calling, about what He has for us. Whether we choose to obey Him or not is a different story.

Looking back, me telling Kabelo I was going to marry Tabatha was the same kind of thing. It wasn't something I planned. It wasn't something I was even thinking about. But it was there. So when I met Tabatha on that cold January night… and when we fell in love so fast… and when we broke up and got back together just as quickly… it all felt like we were walking through something that had already been set in motion.

I *knew* she was the one.

I didn't want to mess this up.

Tabatha would be my wife—just like I had told my friend years before.

part two
THE STORMS WE DIDN'T SEE COMING

four
IS SHE PREGNANT?

I didn't know God very well back then. I believed in Him, but we weren't exactly close. However, I did know one thing—the Bible said that sex before marriage was a sin. Unfortunately, I hadn't really been paying attention to that part. Or, if I did hear it, I was conveniently ignoring it. But something started shifting in our relationship. I started feeling bad about sleeping together.

One day, I messed up. I said, "You know, sweetheart, the Bible says we're not supposed to be having sex before marriage."

I had never heard that before.

I didn't grow up in church. I had only been a few times as a kid, so I didn't know what the Bible actually said. In my mind, if two people loved each other and were in a committed relationship, then God was good with it.

So when Ken said it, I was surprised, but I didn't argue. "Well," I said, "then we don't need to do that anymore." That was it. No back and forth, no debating. In my mind, if it was wrong, then we needed to stop.

But Ken?

Oh yeah. I went into full-time manipulating ninja mode trying to talk her off that ledge. I started pulling out every excuse in the book. "God will forgive us," I told her. "Sin is sin—that's just what people do. But God forgives us, so it's okay."

She was a new believer, so she didn't know how to stand up against my pressure. She gave in. But the conviction didn't go away.

So, one day, I had a bright idea. I called her up and said, "You know what we're going to do? We're going to get married in our hearts. If you come up to my apartment, we'll get on our knees together, and we'll promise God that we'll get married one day. Then, in the eyes of God, we're already married, and we can keep sleeping together."

What was I doing? Making up my own rulebook instead of following His. And isn't that the root of all sin? Choosing what we want more than what He wants?

I was so gullible. Ken could have told me I was a fish, and I would've believed him. I just trusted him. And for me, that was huge. After so much disappointment and betrayal in my past, trust wasn't something I gave away easily. But that butterfly love? Oh, it'll get you.

The truth was—I could make excuses all day, but deep down, I knew they weren't holding up.

I felt it in my spirit. If I loved this woman, I needed to marry her. But let's do the math real quick. We had only been together since January. It was now November.

That's ten months.

And those ten months had been a roller coaster ride—butterfly love, crash and burn, resurrected again, whirlwind emotions. And now, I'm talking about getting married. It sounded crazy, even to me. But I knew what I knew. I believed with all my heart that God was leading me to marry this girl.

So, I called my pastor—Reverend O.T. Moore. He was the senior pastor of New Hope Baptist Church in Beckley, West Virginia, where I grew up. I didn't know a lot about God, but at least I had enough sense to call someone who did.

He lived a few hours away from my college town, but he agreed to meet with me. I pulled up to his house, shook his hand, and sat down on his front porch. With as much sincerity as a 20-year-old could muster, I laid it all out.

"Reverend Moore… there's this girl named Tabatha. I want to marry her, but some people think we're too young. What do you think?"

I thought he was about to give me some long sermon about timing and wisdom, but instead, he asked me two simple questions.

"Have you been together longer than six months?"

"Yes, sir."

"Do you love her?"

"Yes, sir."

"Well, marry her then."

That was it.

I don't know if I'd recommend that advice to just anybody, lol, but for me, it was exactly what I needed to hear. There's safety in the multitude of counselors, but no one can hear God for you. Sometimes, people will say things that don't seem profound, but God will take their advice and make it work for your good in a perfect way. I had a humble heart. I wanted to seek wisdom. And 25 years later, I'm glad I did.

Ring Shopping

Now, it's time to go ring shopping, but I had very little money. I was a junior in college, making next to nothing. I knew I wasn't going to be able to buy her a dream ring, but I had to get something. Around Thanksgiving, I was visiting my parents in Beckley, and I told my friend Tommy, "Man, I want to ask Tabatha to marry me."

He couldn't believe things were moving so fast. Is she pregnant? As the days went on, I'd hear plenty of other people ask the same thing. But, no. That wasn't it at all.

"We're getting married because I believe that's what God told me to do," I'd tell them.

Tommy was all in. He wasn't the kind of friend who was going to try to talk me out of it. He might question it at first, but after that, he was on board. He liked Tabatha. He used to brag that my girlfriend looked like a model.

So, I asked him to come ring shopping with me. I heard that Diamond World was going out of business. That was perfect because I needed a deal. We went inside, and there it was. They had one ring in my price range—$150.

That was all the money I had.

It was a quarter-carat diamond with a black speck in it and some other minor defects. You'd have to look really close to see them.

Without shopping around, without much second-guessing, I said, "I'll take that one."

I had her ring.

I loved that ring. I still have it. And yes, I saw that little black speck from day one, but I never mentioned it. I knew we were in college and broke. So I dreamed of the day he could afford to get me something more.

Besides, in my eyes, the best thing he could give me was him. Everything else was just a cherry on top.

Too many people feel like they have to break the bank to get married. They'll spend $10,000 on a ring, $50,000 on a wedding, and then a few years later, that ring is sitting in a pawn shop somewhere. I would rather spend $150 on a ring, $3,000 on a wedding, and still be married 25 years later.

I always say some people are better at doing weddings than they are at doing marriage. In a perfect world, we'd all have both—a beautiful wedding, a big ring, and a long-lasting marriage.

But if I had to pick, I'd take the marriage 10 out of 10 times.

Christmas Eve Proposal

It was Christmas Eve, 1998. I had asked my parents if I could bring Tabatha home with me for the holidays, and they graciously agreed—on the condition that we sleep in separate rooms. Even though we weren't doing that in college (sorry, Mom), I accepted their request out of respect.

My plan was simple but perfect. I would wait until the clock struck midnight, get down on one knee, and propose.

I remember it like it was yesterday. Tabatha was in blue pajama pants and a t-shirt, just about to turn in for the night. She was staying in my old childhood bedroom, while

I was crammed into the tiny guest room that my mom also used for storage.

A few minutes before midnight, I knocked on her door. I wanted to ease into it, get the conversation going, and wish her a Merry Christmas Eve. Then, at exactly 12:00 AM, I got down on one knee.

"Will you marry me?"

No bands. No videographers. No flashing lights. No fancy dinner. No ring hidden in a cake. Just a young man, trying to obey God and pledge his love to the girl of his dreams.

She had tears in her eyes as she said yes.

We were getting married!

Ken was so sweet. He was also so nervous. I started getting suspicious when he randomly knocked on my door, invited himself in, and started goofing off. It was almost midnight, and this man had energy like it was midday. I thought, What is he up to? When he finally popped the question, I loved the way he did it. Just me and him.

It was perfect. We were together again, and this time I was not letting him go. We had started going to church together, the church where I got baptized. Now that I had this new walk with God, I wanted to live right, and I was thrilled that Ken wanted the same. So when Ken asked me to marry him. I said yes.

Why I didn't tell my parents in advance is beyond me. I think I mentioned it to my dad at some point, but I didn't give them a timeline. So when we woke up on Christmas morning, we had a big announcement to make.

"We're engaged!!!"

My parents were enraged! Sike, just playing. They aren't those kinds of people at all. They hugged us, congratulated us, and celebrated. But I know in the back of their minds, they were probably thinking, This boy is crazy... why didn't he warn us?

But that's just who they are—good, God-fearing, humble-hearted people. Even if they had concerns, they wouldn't have voiced them in a way that was disrespectful to me or Tabatha.

So just like that, we were engaged.

And this was our first official Christmas together.

Oh, that was our first Christmas together! I love Christmas. I'm a Christmas fanatic. Maybe that's why I love it so much—because that Christmas was so special.

Growing up, Christmas was the one holiday when everyone seemed to be happy. There was no fighting, no yelling—just gifts, music, and fun. But Jesus? He wasn't part of our Christmas at all. It was all about Santa Claus.

Then I went to Ken's house and saw his family's Christmas tree. It was beautifully decorated, but what stood out to me the most was the ribbon flowing down the sides that said, Happy Birthday, Jesus.

That was the first time it hit me—Christmas was actually about celebrating the birth of Jesus. Who knew?! And then, as if Christmas couldn't get any better, Ken went and made it even better. December 25th, 1998, at exactly 12:00am, became our official engagement date.

I Do

We set the wedding date for July 3rd, 1999. My friends weren't shocked at me getting engaged, but they were shocked at me setting a wedding date. We heard of people getting engaged as they were getting ready to graduate college, but not a lot were going to get married while in college. I'll admit, that is something I probably wouldn't recommend. But we had conviction. And although there were a lot of side comments, and disapproving looks going around, no one dared to tell us not to do it. So we did it.

Since Tabatha's father had passed away when she was six, and she didn't want to put any financial burden on her mom, we decided to have the wedding in Beckley, West Virginia, where I grew up.

We seriously considered just going to the courthouse. But something inside of me said, No—we need to do this in God's house. Honor God and honor our families.

I've never liked being the center of attention. I love throwing a party for other people, but I don't love them for myself. So when it came to getting married, I honestly would've been fine with going to the courthouse and making it legal. I thought, It's just between me and him—we don't need anyone else there.

Of course, I would've loved to have a big, beautiful wedding, but I wasn't willing to go broke or crazy trying to make it happen. Ken convinced me otherwise. He came from a great family, and he wanted to honor them and God by allowing them to be part of this moment. And he was right. I just didn't know how big of a deal a wedding really was or how important it was for family to be there.

So we chose to get married at New Hope Baptist Church. This was the church that raised me. I got baptized there. I went to funerals there. I sang in the children's choir there. This church was my foundation.

And the wedding was happening fast.

We weren't waiting for people to fund it or plan it—we were getting married because we believed it was what God wanted us to do. The total cost was around $3,000, and most of it ended up on my credit card, adding to the financial trouble that would come knocking later.

We also decided not to have alcohol at the wedding. For us, alcohol represented a life we wanted to leave behind. Tabatha grew up in an addictive environment. She had addictive tendencies. When she failed out of school, she spent nights drinking her sorrows away. I remember when we were dating and I would come home to find her passed out in my bathroom, sleeping next to the toilet because she was so drunk. I'd try to pick her up and move her to the bed, but she'd be completely out of it.

I fully understand that for some people growing up drinking a glass of wine with dinner or a half of glass of wine here and there without overindulging was a part of their culture. But that isn't our story. If Tabatha was drinking, she was drinking to get drunk.

For me, drinking was more of a social thing. I wasn't a heavy drinker, but I knew that nothing good ever came from it. My judgment would be off, I'd say and do stupid stuff, and most of my drinking was tied to a life I was trying to leave behind. So, when we decided to get married, we knew—alcohol wasn't going to be a part of it.

And boy were we were persecuted for that! In college, we were the life of the party. I threw legendary house parties with trash cans full of jungle juice—Kool-Aid, fruit pieces, and 190-proof grain alcohol mixed together to get people lit. I drank Mad Dog, Cisco, vodka, Roman Cokes, White Russians—you name it. People knew me for throwing parties where folks would be passed out from drugs or alcohol, and we'd just keep partying the night away.

So when we told our friends that there would be no reception and no alcohol at our wedding, people thought we were trippin.' Some of them didn't even come. And that's okay.

Whenever you try to do something for God, some people will be for you, and some will be against you. We saw our wedding as a symbol of God's doing, and we didn't want to bring anything into our new marriage that didn't honor Him. So instead of a reception, we just had some food in the basement of the church after the ceremony.

But here's the thing—the hallmark of a Christian Atheist is that we know just enough to feel bad about what we're doing, but not enough to stop doing what we know is wrong. So while we took a bold stance against having alcohol at the wedding, the night before the wedding? Let's just say it was a different story.

Wait a minute. Before we get too far in his pre-wedding exploits, let me just say that unlike my freaky husband, I told my friends I did not want to have the traditional bachelorette party. In fact the night before our wedding, I went to sleep. I was not interested in drinking or nasty naked men and my friends knew it. I can be quite stern when I believe in something. I'm sure a couple of them thought I was coo-coo for Coco Puffs because I had changed so drastically. I was not the same Tabatha they met freshman year. When I met Jesus, my heart changed. Although, I couldn't express it yet, God was working in me. I didn't know why, but I didn't want to do the things I used to do. I wanted to please God and that made me happy.

Okay, fine. When Tabatha got saved, she really got saved. I, on the other hand, needed a little work. Me and some of my wedding party were out making it rain at Southern Exposure—a strip club in southern West Virginia. And let me just say, the name Southern Exposure was literal in more ways than one.

See, the problem with this kind of double life is that the Bible calls it being lukewarm. And lukewarm is a dangerous place to be. God says He'd rather us be hot or cold, but lukewarm? That's the same as cold in His eyes.

But back then, I didn't know any better. I lived my life by what was popular, what was socially acceptable, and what everybody else did. And everybody knew that a bachelor party was just what you did—one last wild night before getting hitched.

I won't go into details about that night, but while it wasn't as bad as The Hangover Part 1, 2, or 3 movies, it was a long way from holiness and godliness. As believers, it's so important that we don't get lost in the cultural norms of a secular society. It's okay to stand up and say, "No, I'm not going to that bachelor party." It's okay to say, "Let's celebrate, but naked men and women who aren't mine is

NOT the way I want to do it." It's okay to be counterculture and take a stand.

Unfortunately, I wasn't like Tabatha. I didn't take that stand. I compromised, and I didn't realize that these small cracks in my integrity would eventually come back to haunt our young marriage.

Because 24 hours later—Tabatha's last name changed, the date on the calendar changed…

But my mindset hadn't.

And the truth is, the problems in a marriage? They don't start after the wedding. If you look closely, you can see them before you ever say, "I do."

I am so thankful for the people who helped make our wedding happen. We didn't have a huge budget, but what we lacked in funds, our family and friends made up for in love and generosity.

My mom and dad pitched in a lot. Tabatha's mom and family worked hard, cooking most of the food for the gathering after the wedding. Friends and family came together to decorate, rent tuxes, and set up everything for the ceremony. It wasn't fancy or extravagant, but it was ours.

When I think about that day, I don't remember what we didn't have. I remember who showed up. I remember the people who believed in us, who supported two broke college students making a bold decision to honor God and commit to each other for life.

And for that, I will forever be grateful.

Forever grateful indeed! Ken's mom practically planned the whole wedding. She hired a wedding planner, bought the wedding cake, and even typed up the programs. My entire family showed up, driving three to four hours from Pennsylvania. My mom brought food, my sister and brother were in the ceremony, and my friends were there to celebrate.

I remember looking around at the packed church in shock. I had no idea so many people cared. After struggling with low self-esteem, depression, and suicidal thoughts for most of my life, I never imagined people would show up for me like that.

That little church held about 250 people—I think. If that's the case, it felt like we had 255 people squeezed in there. I come from a huge family, and they showed up big for us. My uncle Greg officiated the wedding, which was really special for me. Growing up, he was the one who taught me how to swim, and he was always someone I looked up to. But that day? That day, all I saw was sweat.

It was July 3rd, the middle of summer, and of all days, that was the day the church's air conditioning decided to give up on life. I had never seen people sweat like that. I mean, it was miserable, but hey—the show must go on. Uncle Greg stood at the altar, bible in one hand, officiating the ceremony like a true man of God. But let me tell you, I couldn't focus on a single word he was saying because sweat was rolling off that chocolate bald head of his like a waterfall. His bible was soaking wet—I mean, this brother's pages were stuck together! I wanted to laugh so bad... but I held it in. Barely.

For me, that day was far from glamorous.

Yes, people had come together to celebrate me, but somehow, I still felt like I had to take care of everyone else. I was running around, making sure everybody had what they needed, that they looked great, that they were put together. And what did that leave for me? No time to get myself together. I wanted to be a beautiful bride, walking down the aisle, but I felt far from it.

I was sending people to Walmart because they forgot their shirts. My hair was a disaster, my makeup was melting off my face, and to top it all off, my bouquet smelled like old weeds. The final straw? The person who was supposed to walk me down the aisle was a no-show. The little girl inside me wanted to run away and cry. I wished my daddy were alive to give me away to the man of my dreams. But my life had never been a fairy tale, and I had long since learned how to fend for myself.

So, I did what I always did. I walked into a bathroom stall, locked the door, and gave myself a pep talk. "All that matters is that I am marrying the man I love. Today, I become Mrs. Ken Claytor, and that's all that matters." I took a deep breath, put on my strongest face and my brightest smile, and walked myself down that aisle.

And then I saw her.

And just like that, the worries faded away.

She was beautiful, kind, had a brilliant mind, loved God, and most importantly—she wanted to marry me. Our wedding colors were periwinkle and white. Our wedding song was "All My Life" by K-Ci and JoJo. We weren't playing. We meant every single word.

In truth, I was in over my head. I didn't know what the future held for me. I was a baby Christian. I didn't have all the answers. I was scared. But I was brave enough to follow my heart and follow God. And that was enough. I didn't know where the road would take us, but I had someone to walk it with me. And I think that was the key.

We had so many issues to overcome. But we just kept taking steps. One step at a time. Toward God. Toward each other. Toward our future.

Uncle Greg led us through our vows. I didn't write my own, and honestly? I don't even remember what was said. Another red flag. I was just going through the motions, trying to get through the ceremony so we could get out of this hot church and get on with our honeymoon in the Poconos.

We got married on July 3, 1999 but I was not a husband on July 3, 1999. Shoot—I wasn't even a man yet. Just like me, so many people walk into marriage not knowing how to be a husband or wife. We stand at that altar, reciting vows we don't fully understand, making lifelong commitments we have no idea how to keep. We think love will be enough—but love, by itself, isn't enough.

Our wedding was beautiful. We had great food at the reception—fried chicken and cake. My kind of eating.

And then, just as we were leaving the church, the sky opened up, and it poured rain.

I mean, it rained hard.

I wonder… was that a sign? A sign of showers of blessings? Or a sign of the storms that would come?

Only time would tell…

five
THE HONEYMOON IS OVER

We always tell couples—before you say "I do," the real question you should be asking is "Do I?" So many people rush into marriage, swept up in the romance of the moment, without ever stopping to ask themselves: Do I?

Do I understand what it truly means to be a godly husband or wife? Do I commit to them my unfailing love, no matter what comes or goes? Do I have the stamina and strength to love through all seasons—financial shortages or abundance, successes and failures, sickness and health?

We know all of these seasons all too well.

Not writing my own vows is one thing. But not even remembering what in the world I said that day? That's something else entirely. Like so many people, I was just going through the motions, walking down a path without really knowing where it led. And if we were honest, we could have seen the cracks in our foundation long ago. The butterflies have a way of putting carpet over the cracks so that you don't even realize they're still there.

If you really think about our love story, it sounds like something straight out of a romantic comedy or a fairy tale. Guy sees girl. Girl is with someone else. Guy waits patiently for girl. Girl breaks up with the other guy. Guy gets the girl. They fall "drunk in love" with passion and romance. And they live happily ever after.

At least… that's what happens in the movies.

But life? Life isn't a movie. And neither is marriage. We are real people, with a real past, facing real problems, that require real solutions. Looking back, the red flags were there all along.

Now, red flags aren't necessarily deal breakers. But they are things you need to pay attention to before moving on to the next phase of the relationship. There is no such thing as marrying a perfect person, but there are certain qualities that can prevent major fallouts later. A red flag simply means proceed with caution.

But whatever you do—don't ignore the red flags.

Ha. My middle name was red flag. My whole existence should have been a flashing neon warning sign for you. The heavy drinking, dropping out of school, joining the military, my troubled family life, the depression—it was all there. How did either of us survive in this relationship?

But God. Seriously, unless you're working with God, you're working in vain. I'm not saying God came down from heaven and magically fixed our marriage. No, we absolutely had to do the work. I just say that to give hope to couples in difficult marriages. It's easy to think it's too late for you, that you've already ignored too many red flags to recover. But if our story shows anything, it's that even when you've ignored all the red flags—and then some—it's still possible to make it. Here we are, all these years later, and we're still together. If that's not proof of what God can do, I don't know what is.

There were tons of red flags in our beautiful love story. Tabatha was already engaged in college—what kind of relationship was that? Was it controlling? Was it abusive? How had it affected and infected her heart and perspectives on future love? Then there was me—I was very comfortable around women. I had tons of female friends and a little bit of a reputation for being a player. Could I be faithful? Could I commit to one woman? Could I be trusted?

Tabatha was out of school and unsure of her future. She didn't know where she was going or how she would get there. She lacked vision and direction. She was also a heavy drinker, and alcohol made her more lovable, but could this become a problem? On top of that, she was battling depression and in therapy—would she be able to come out of it? How would this impact our marriage and future together? She had experienced an overwhelming amount of trauma—sexual abuse, physical abuse, rejection, and abandonment. How would that affect our relationship moving forward?

We were both broke. Financial pressure is one of the leading causes of divorce, so how would that affect our marriage? And then, we were super young. Not that you have to be older to be married, but we didn't even know who we were yet, nor what we wanted in a spouse. On top of all that, we didn't have a church home or spiritual mentoring. We were just living life based on our own rules. Marriage is ministry, and if it's ministry, there will be warfare. If there's warfare, you need spiritual covering—and we didn't have that.

Then there were the red flags that weren't as obvious. Like how I dealt with bitterness and betrayal. A part of my personality is that I will let you in, but if you cross me, I don't want much to do with you after that. I wasn't quick to "turn the other cheek" after our breakup. Then, there were the religious blinders we had on. I had a conviction that "God said," but I had no real understanding of what obeying God would cost me. I was blindly obeying Him, which is a good thing, but I was not expecting the kind of warfare I was going to experience because of it.

Tabatha had never seen a loving marriage before. All our friends were single. Neither one of us had many godly friends at all. And then, there was the fact that Tabatha would hide things from me if she was embarrassed about them. For example, she hid the fact that she smoked cigarettes. I personally had never seen her smoke before, and she didn't admit it until years into our marriage.

I did hide cigarette smoking from Ken. It was gross, but I loved the nicotine high. I was a social smoker. My girls and I would go out to the club, drink, dance, and when we wanted a cigarette break, we'd give the signal and all meet in the ladies' room to share cigarettes. I learned from my grandma to stash things away in my brassiere. They'd be waiting for me in the restroom because I had the cigarettes and lighter, along with my ID, lipstick, and cash all tucked into my bosom. None of us wanted to be seen smoking, so it was our little secret.

So, when we say the honeymoon was over, we're not just talking about getting back from the Poconos. I mean the *butterfly feeling* was over. The infatuation stage had ended. Now we were in the middle. Now we were in conflict. What would we do?

The First Two Years

The first two years of our marriage were rough, to say the least. We loved each other, but we've learned that love alone isn't always enough to keep a marriage together. We didn't know how to talk or communicate with each other. We didn't know how to build trust. We didn't know how to discuss sex. We didn't know how to divide responsibilities or rely on the Holy Spirit to lead us. We didn't know how to go to God's Word for answers or direction. We didn't know how to handle conflict. Truthfully, we didn't know a lot.

I knew marriage wouldn't be easy, but I didn't think it would feel like this. I was fighting a battle with depression, and I had hoped marriage would help make me whole. But instead, it exposed my brokenness. It forced me to see how unhealed I really was. And it forced Ken to see it, too. We were two people in love but lost at the same time. I was trying to find my way out of depression, and he was trying to find his way out of the house.

It felt strange from the beginning. I remember putting on that wedding ring for the first time. It was like I had a spotlight on my hand, like it was glowing—almost like Luke Skywalker's lightsaber from *Star Wars*. I don't know if this was just a *me* thing or a *man* thing, but wearing a wedding band at 21 years old just felt... weird.

I don't remember feeling weird about my wedding ring. I was too focused on just making it through the day. Depression has a way of making everything feel like a blur. It steals the joy out of things that should be beautiful. I wanted to be happy. I wanted to feel like a newlywed. But I just felt... tired. Exhausted from carrying the weight of my own mind. And I don't know if Ken even realized how bad it was for me.

We got married the summer before our senior year of college and rented a small house for $350 a month. It was a perfect little spot for newlyweds. We could walk to class, had a yard, and even a big wooden deck for cookouts. But even in that perfect setup, we struggled. I struggled to pay rent—even though it was only $350 a month. And we struggled emotionally, especially as Tabatha's depression crept back in. Our butterfly love had covered it up for a while, but now we were forced to face reality.

The house should have been perfect, but it didn't feel like home. I was still trying to figure out who I was, and suddenly, I was supposed to be someone's wife. But how could I be a wife when I barely felt like a person? Some days I felt present, but most days, I was in survival mode. Ken would go out with his friends, and I'd be home alone, with no energy, barely aware that he was even gone.

The reality was that I was not yet a faithful man in my heart, and she was not yet healed enough to be a wife. So there we were, stuck in this house together, sharing a last name, but feeling like something was *off.*

There were times I would go out with my friends, trying to reclaim the freedom I had before marriage. I'd take my ring off, just to feel like one of the guys again, to talk to women the way I used to. Tabatha's friends knew she was home while I was out, and they tried to warn her about me. They told her she shouldn't trust me, that I wasn't being the husband I had promised to be.

I didn't need my friends to tell me what I already knew. Ken was struggling. And I was struggling. We were just struggling in different ways. I coped by withdrawing, by shutting down. He coped by escaping, by running toward the world he knew before me. I could feel the distance growing between us, but I didn't know how to stop it. And honestly? I didn't know if I had the strength to try.

One night at a club, I was out with my friends and ended up dancing with this girl from my business class. She was the type to sit in the front row, take notes, never socialize. But that night? She had her hair down, her glasses off, and was dancing like I had never seen before. It was like when Ms. Westlake from *The Cosby Show* let loose—you suddenly saw her in a different light. I was caught off guard. One thing led to another, and we decided to leave together.

I told her to meet me on a certain street, and I picked her up. We went back to her place, started making out, and then I felt it—that deep conviction. Like, Man, what am I doing? But she wasn't stopping. She leaned in and said, "I can keep a secret. I won't tell." She knew I was married, but she didn't care. In that moment, I came to myself. I got out of there. There was no sex, but let's be clear—that was still cheating. I had no business being there.

And I wish I could say that was the only time something like that happened. But it wasn't. Cancun was another mistake, another poor decision that I justified in my mind. My friends invited me on a guys' trip, and I convinced myself that this would be my last chance to have fun before I fully committed to being a husband—as if I wasn't already married.

The trip was a disaster. We partied recklessly. My friend fell off a stage while dancing and broke his arm. I danced and partied with women who weren't my wife. I didn't go all the way, but I did things I had no business doing. I convinced myself it wasn't that bad because there was no sex, but that's a lie. There are things that are meant to be only between a husband and a wife. I broke that.

When I got home, Tabatha met me at the door. She was loving, kind, and had missed me—even though I had just spent a week in Cancun doing God knows what. She never asked questions, never accused me. I think she *knew* I wasn't all the way there yet. And somehow, she always handled it with grace.

I didn't ask questions because I didn't want to know the answers. I had nothing left to give. The slightest trouble could trigger a panic attack where I would become overwhelmed, hyperventilate, and become physically immobile. I kept the panic attacks a secret from Ken. I didn't want him to know how broken I was. But after getting married, I wanted to be free from depression more than ever before. I was so determined to overcome depression that I put all of my focus on fighting it. Which meant, I didn't have the mental capacity to fight with my husband or worse, for my husband.

I was going to weekly counseling sessions and for the first time, diving deeply into my scary past. I admitted to being molested for the very first time. I went toe-to-toe with abuse from my childhood. It took bravery, vulnerability, and a whole lot of mental fortitude. Ken had to feel neglected, even lonely. I emotionally abandoned him. The nurturing Tabatha who showered him with love and affection was no longer available. Not to justify it, but some of what he did could have been cries for attention because he wasn't getting any from me. I had an inkling that he was unfaithful, but I just didn't want to see it. I just didn't have the mental capacity to handle that piece of information. My plate was full.

Even though I was young and foolish, I wasn't heartless. I knew what we had was real. I had a vision for our future. I just didn't know how to deal with the gap between where we were and where I wanted us to be. I didn't know how to deal with the difficulties and responsibilities of being a husband. I didn't know how to deal with the pressures of being the only married couple among my friends.

God had told us to get married, but it would take years for me to truly become the husband I was supposed to be. But thankfully, I would get there.

The Graduation

The time had finally come for us to graduate. I was looking forward to getting out of college, starting our careers, and making a fresh start in a new city. But we had a problem. Tabatha's depression had made it hard for her to keep up in classes, and we were told that if she failed even one class this last semester, she wouldn't graduate.

Right before graduation, we found out that she was, in fact, going to fail a class. I was livid. I felt like I had been carrying dead weight around, and this was the last straw. I was ambitious, determined to make something of myself, and I started believing the lie that I had made a mistake marrying her. I heard the voices of people who had warned us before we got married: You're too young. This isn't right. You're rushing into something you're not ready for.

I told myself that if she didn't graduate, I was leaving. I was moving to Washington, D.C., without her. There were no online classes back then. She wouldn't be able to transfer. In my mind, I was already gone.

I knew the temperature of my husband's heart. He was leaving Morgantown, with or without me. I could feel it in the way he looked at me, in the way he barely spoke to me. I had disappointed him, again. But I didn't know what else to do. I tried so hard to pass my classes, but my brain felt like a fog of clouds and tweety birds. I couldn't concentrate. I couldn't retain information. I could barely stay awake to study. And now, it was all coming down to this one class. Geography. Of all things.

When I started making plans to leave, part of me knew it was wrong. The Bible says in Matthew 19:6, "What therefore God has joined together, let not man separate." And I think He meant what He said. It's never good to make plans to separate. It does something destructive to your soul. When two become one, trying to become two again is not easy. Looking back, I don't know what I would have done. Maybe I would have tried long distance for a while. But make no mistake—I was gone. My bags were packed, the truck was running. At least, that's how I saw it.

So, I did the only thing I knew to do when facing an impossible situation—I prayed. This was the second big prayer I remember asking God for. I asked Him to make a way for me to graduate because I wanted to go with my husband. That was it. I had nothing else but a prayer and a sliver of hope. I went to the records office, heart pounding, hoping for a miracle. I asked if I was on the graduation list. A voice called out from behind a partition, "What's your name?" It felt like a scene from The Wizard of Oz, like the great and powerful wizard himself was deciding my fate. I took a deep breath. "Tabatha Claytor." There was a long pause. Then, from behind the curtain, the voice shouted, "Congratulations! You're on the list."

Ken was furious. "How can you graduate if you failed a class?" He actually started to convince me that I wasn't supposed to graduate, that there had to be some mistake. And honestly? I was already so used to doubting myself that I almost believed him. But I held on to what I knew: the lady told me I was on the list. That was all I had. I couldn't explain it. I couldn't defend it. I just knew that I had prayed, and God had answered.

The day of graduation was supposed to be a celebration, but for us, it was nothing but stress. We weren't even sure why we were there. Something in us must have been holding on to hope, believing in a ram in the bush before we even knew what that meant. Tabatha put on her cap and gown, and we went through the whole ceremony without knowing if she had actually graduated.

I was angry. My parents were there. We had sat through the entire graduation, but in the back of my mind, I kept thinking, "She failed a class. How is she even here?" I still didn't believe what she'd said from the record's office.

So, after the ceremony, we had to go to the tent where they handed out actual degrees. I knew. This is when reality is really going to hit.

Everything slowed down. I watched as Tabatha walked up to the table. The administrator asked for her name. "Tabatha Claytor," she said. The woman scanned the files, and my heart was pounding. Then, to my shock, she pulled out a degree. "Congratulations," she said, handing it to her. And just like that, Tabatha walked off, diploma in hand.

To this day, we don't know how she graduated. But we've got two degrees hanging on our wall, and that's all that matters. People ask me all the time, "If God is real, why doesn't He show us a sign?" And I always tell them—there are signs everywhere if you just open your eyes. If you want to see a sign, come over to our house. I'll show you a college degree on the wall that wasn't supposed to be there. There's your sign.

I am so thankful for the grace of God. He knew what we needed. We needed to get out of Morgantown. Away from our friends. Away from the college life. We needed a fresh start, a new place where He could begin working on us as a couple. That place, for us, was Washington, D.C.

It was our promised land.

But just like in the Bible, we were about to find out— the Promised Land still had giants that needed to be defeated.

six
BYE-BYE BUTTERFLIES

After graduating from West Virginia University in 2000, we moved to the Washington, D.C., area. By the grace of God, we moved together and not separately. I had a few job offers come in—from Beneficial as a financial advisor, Enterprise Rent-A-Car as a sales rep, and Hecht's department store working in Human Resources. The pay range of those offers was between $26,000 and $37,500 a year. But when we added up our student loans, credit cards, and other debts, we owed over $100,000. We didn't own a home, and we had one old car that we were still paying off.

I felt an incredible amount of financial pressure in those first two years of marriage—so much that I remember waking up some mornings in tears, feeling like we were never going to find our way to financial freedom. So, I did what made the most sense to me: I took the highest-paying job offer to relieve some of that pressure. It was $37,500 working for Hecht's corporate office in Baltimore, Maryland. One problem, though—we had just signed a lease in Arlington, Virginia. With no traffic, that was an hour-long drive one way.

As my start date approached, I had a nagging feeling I just couldn't shake. I didn't want to go. It didn't feel right. And because I was immature at the time, I didn't even show up. I called them a day later and said, "I just can't come." No backup plan, no strategy—just a gut feeling that I wasn't supposed to be there.

When we got to Washington, D.C., I thought, "Yes, I made it!" I was just glad to be with my husband. Not to mention, it was Washington, D.C.! This girl from the country projects was excited. I had taken road trips to D.C. and New York City in college, but I had only dreamed about actually living in a major city. It felt like there was so much opportunity ahead of us.

I had no idea Ken was so stressed about our finances. I had been poor my whole life, so financial pressures didn't bother me. It was just life. Growing up, we didn't pay the bills on purpose because once you got far enough behind, you qualified for financial assistance that covered everything. We got a check on the third of the month, cashed it, and spent it the same day. There was no savings, no plan—just trying to make a dollar out of fifteen cents.

You'd think I would've picked up some good financial habits in college, but I didn't. I studied Economics 101, but I knew nothing about budgeting, balancing a checkbook, or saving. I learned the hard way. When I started applying for jobs, they wanted to check my credit score. So before I could even get a decent job, I had to clean up my credit report. Ugh. That was humbling and eye-opening. Between making phone calls to creditors and arguing with Ken a billion times about money, I finally got it. Let's just say I "adulted." Hey, but I did learn. My credit score has been excellent for years now.

This is what I knew: making $26,000 to $37,500 a year wasn't going to cut it. Not with this kind of debt. I needed a way to make more money and have a shorter commute. I thought to myself, I need to own a business. I had gone to school for business, and I had always been entrepreneurial. But I needed capital, and I had none. My second thought? Sales. Sales is all commission, but at least there's no income ceiling. I figured I could sell cars, planes, or homes. Since I didn't know anyone selling planes or how to get into that industry, I decided to sell homes. Real estate made sense. Houses cost more than cars, and if I was going to work on commission, I might as well sell something with a higher price tag. I also wanted to flip homes and build apartment buildings, so learning real estate from the inside out seemed like the best move.

I was down for the hustle. I had started working at fourteen years old. All through college, I worked—sometimes juggling work-study jobs, part-time jobs, and a full-time class schedule. So, I was ready to get to work. I took a sales job walking business to business selling postage products. It promised quick money, and I figured it would hold me over until I found something stable.

Within a month or so, I got two stable offers. Ken, who is still the best negotiator I know, gave me great tips on how to negotiate my salary. I accepted a position at an HR firm as an administrative assistant, making $35,000 a year plus full benefits (which, back in 2000, was great). I was thrilled. I worked in a high-rise building. I wore suits and high heels to work. I was determined to succeed. I was on my way.

While Tabatha worked full-time, I pursued my real estate license, and we lived off her salary alone. I made some extra money painting houses on the side. A friend from West Virginia had moved to D.C. around the same time we did, and his cousin's husband was a painter. They let us stay with them for the first few weeks in D.C., and the husband gave me a job painting houses with him. I mainly painted doors while the other guys handled the more intricate work, but that extra couple hundred dollars here and there helped a lot.

It was a tough time, but at least we were in the game. We were in a new city, pursuing our careers, and that helped ease some tension. But all wasn't well. Tabatha still battled depression. We still didn't know how to have a "better marriage." And I was still straddling the fence when it came to faithfulness.

One day, I was at Office Depot, picking up supplies for work, and I saw this really cute girl. She looked like she might have worked there. I walked up, got her name, and asked for her number. With my wedding ring shining bright, she knew I was married—but she gave me her number anyway. Things at home were okay, but not good. We were distant, and I just needed someone to talk to. So I called her.

"Hello, can I speak to—"

"This is her," she said. Then, without hesitation, she added, "Cheating already, huh? I tell you, y'all are no good."

She still entertained the conversation, but her tone said everything. It wasn't shock or disappointment. It was more like, this is just the way guys are. Like she figured if it wasn't her, it'd be someone else.

That conversation was short, but I'll tell you this—I didn't want to feel that way anymore. I didn't want to be a cheater. I didn't want to be an adulterer. I didn't want to be talking to other women. I just didn't know how to talk to mine.

Yikes. I was oblivious to Ken's schemes once we got to D.C. I was so busy with my new job, I didn't notice. Professionally, I was learning so much, but I was also growing as a person. I went from learning how to use a fax machine to running software programs. Attending company functions, networking, and learning how to navigate office meetings were all stretching me. I was learning how to enter a room, when to speak, when to keep silent, how to dress for success, how to strategize and collaborate. I felt good about what I was doing at work.

But when I came home, well... that was a different story.

Those first two years were rough. I would shut down and give Tabatha the silent treatment for days at a time. I'd leave the house and threaten not to come back. I was mean. When we argued, if I did decide to come to bed at night, I would sleep on the edge of the mattress—literally on the seam. I didn't want to see her, I didn't want to hear from her, and I didn't want her to even know I cared. Looking back, I don't think any of it worked. She seemed oblivious to what I was going through. Wisdom key: manipulation never works.

On a scale from 1 to 10, I'd rate our marriage a 3. We had some good times in there. She was still sweet, still caring. I was still me. But our relationship wasn't healthy. I meditated on divorce, I threatened divorce, and at one point, I actually started planning for it.

At this point, I didn't think our relationship was that bad. I would've given it a 7. That probably sounds crazy, but my perspective back then was skewed. For most of my life, I had seen men be unfaithful, bouncing from one baby mama to another, or they were abusive—physically, verbally, or emotionally. I knew Ken was no angel, but he wasn't out getting another woman pregnant, and he had never put his hands on me. Those were pretty low standards, but that's where I was. I settled for less because I didn't know there was more.

At the peak of it all, I remember calling my dad and telling him I wanted a divorce. I said, "Dad, Tabatha doesn't do this, she doesn't do that, she doesn't—"

He cut me off with a two-letter prophetic word that changed my life.

"So?"

That's it. That's all he said. And I guess that's all he needed to say. What I heard in that was, So what? Stop making a mountain out of a molehill. So what, she's not your slave? So what, she doesn't do everything exactly how you want? So what, grow up. This is till death do you part.

Nobody made you get up on that altar and get married. This was your decision.

God was using little moments like this to help me see the truth. It's easy to blame your spouse for where you are in your marriage. That's classic blame-shifting and low-level understanding. But the truth was, I had a bigger role in our dysfunction than I wanted to admit.

Back then, I thought Tabatha was 70% of the problem, and I maybe made up 30%—if that. Looking back now, it was 70% me and 30% her. I just couldn't see it at the time. And that's the problem with people who are ready to walk away from their marriage. They're blinded by blame. The road to recovery starts with realizing that you have a huge role to play in where your marriage is today. You have to own that.

I wish I could've just read the Bible and gotten that message. I wish I could've just heard it from a pastor or a wise counselor. But my life wasn't there yet. So God used whatever He could to get my attention—random girls at Office Depot, women who made me uncomfortable by saying, "I can keep a secret," and a no-nonsense father who only needed one word to check me.

Little did I know that God was about to move me into a season of more direct and precise communication with Him. My world was about to change.

I can see now that my struggle with depression blinded me from seeing the problems in my marriage. I was completely out of touch with what was happening in Ken's world. How can you own up to your part when you don't even know something's wrong?

Thankfully for us, things were about to change.

I Like Cake

September 11, 2001 shook our nation. It was a time of mourning for the lives lost in the terrorist attacks, but it was also a time of great unity. I had never seen our country pull together across racial and political lines like that before. People were proud to be American. At the time of the attacks, we were living in Upper Marlboro, Maryland—about a 30-minute drive from the Pentagon. That morning, Tabatha was at the gym in Largo, just ten minutes from our house, and I was sitting at home, eating a bowl of cereal and watching TV.

I looked up and saw a plane crash into a building. By the screams coming through the television, I could tell this wasn't a movie. It was real.

By this time, we had a cell phone, so I called my wife and said, "Sweetie, something's happening. I think you should come home."

As I continued watching, I saw the second plane hit the second tower—live. The screams, the chaos—it was like something out of a nightmare.

And then, a little later, the news reported that a plane had crashed into the Pentagon. That one shook me. Not just because we lived 30 minutes away at the time, but because, months earlier, we had lived right near the Pentagon. When we first moved to the D.C. area, we stayed on Columbia Pike in Arlington, Virginia. I used to jog around the Pentagon all the time for exercise. It was surreal to think an attack of that magnitude had hit so close to home.

This attack was sobering. It made us all reflect on the value of life and what really mattered.

I was at the gym when it happened. One of the trainers turned the TV up and told us to come see what was going on. It felt like the world had stopped. Nobody was talking. Nobody was moving. We all just stood there, staring at the screen, watching smoke rise from the Twin Towers. I felt numb. I grabbed my bag and left immediately, heading home to Ken. When I pulled into the driveway, I found him sitting in front of the TV, shaking his head, his bowl of cereal barely touched.

That was the first time I had ever really considered how fragile life was. How everything can change in a moment. It made me think: If something happened to me today, where would I go? Was I ready?

Around the same time, I met a new real estate client. I had been in real estate for about a year at that point, but I just couldn't get good traction. I started in commercial real estate but was about to transition to residential because the money came quicker there.

This particular couple didn't have much buying power, but they were looking by faith. And since I had time, I was willing to walk with them through the process in hopes that they'd buy something in the future.

One day, after seeing houses, they invited me to their church. But they didn't just invite me—they gave me a cake.

They said, "Would you like to come to church with us?" and handed me a pound cake with icing on it. Anyone who knows me knows I love cake. I smiled and said, "Sure. When and where?" They told me about a special Tuesday night service. I had never heard of people going to church on a Tuesday night, but I liked the couple. And I liked cake. So, I went.

Much to my surprise, the church was packed. Thousands of people were there. It was so full that the couple who invited us got there early just to save us seats. When we arrived, they waved us over.

The moment we stepped inside, I knew this was different. There were TV cameras and big screens in the sanctuary. People were excited, almost like they were about to watch a game or a concert. They smiled and hugged us like they actually cared. I wasn't used to that. I had grown up in churches of 40, maybe 100 people at most. This church had 1,500 in the main auditorium alone, not even counting the overflow rooms.

The guest minister that night made a request. "If you're here and you want to give $1,000 to the Lord, please stand." Now, I had always considered myself a generous person. I loved the Lord from what I knew about Him. I had been the guy to give $20 in the offering when others gave a dollar or two. So, I didn't think much about it. Of course, I wanted to give God $1,000!

The problem was—I didn't have $1,000 to my name. I also didn't know that he wanted us to give it that night. But all I heard was, "Do you want to give?" and I thought, Absolutely. So, I stood up. I believed God saw my heart. He always sees our hearts. That's what He wants more than anything else. The preacher then said, "If you're standing, please come to the front." At that moment, I grabbed Tabatha's hand—maybe my first sign of spiritual leadership—and said, "Let's go."

As we approached the front of the church, the preacher began to line people up on the front of the altar in a line going from left to right in front of the platform. Then he began to pray for people. But he didn't just pray for people. He started at the far end of the line, and as he prayed for people I saw them fall backwards.

As a young man who grew in a small protestant mainline denominational church, I had never seen or experienced anything like that. But I had seen that happen on TV before and subconsciously concluded that wasn't for me. So, I had this thought before he began to pray for us, "I am not falling down" in here. I also remember kind of planting my feet like I am not falling, and he is not pushing me down. Don't know why I felt that way, that was just my response.

I was definitely an innocent bystander in this whole situation. First of all, I thought it was weird that Ken's clients gave him a cake. I didn't eat it because I didn't know them. Could've been a poison cake for all I knew. But Ken ate the whole thing.

Then, when we pulled up to this church, I was flipping through our MapQuest printout, double-checking the address. It didn't even look like a church. There were cars everywhere. We had to park blocks away and walk. When we got inside, the place was packed. There were no empty seats. But Ken's clients had saved us a spot—in the front.

Then, out of nowhere, Ken stands up talking about giving $1,000. I'm thinking, With what money? And before I knew it, the preacher called all the people standing to the front. Ken grabbed my hand and pulled me with him. I was fussing the whole way up. "Ken! Ken!" And he was like, "Come on, Tab!"

I had no idea what was going on. The next thing I knew, this preacher was touching people's foreheads, and they were passing out! I had seen this kind of thing on TV, and I was not having it. I was from the hood. I was ready to fight.

But then something happened. Something I couldn't explain. I felt something in the room, around me, inside me. I wanted to run, but I also wanted to stay. A thought popped into my mind—what if this is real? What if this is what I've been searching for?

I stood at the altar with my knees locked, ready for whatever was about to happen next. The preacher touched my forehead, and suddenly, my knees buckled. My legs gave out beneath me. I fell to the floor. For a moment, it felt like time slowed down. The sound around me became muffled. I knew—this was real.

I wasn't down for long. As soon as I could, I jumped back up to my feet. I looked around for Ken, and just as I thought he had left me up there, I looked down and saw him… still lying on the floor. His eyes were closed. And I thought, "Get up, Ken! Why won't he get up?!"

As the preacher moved toward us, I was holding Tabatha's hand. He hadn't even touched me yet, but I felt this overwhelming presence come over me. My knees buckled, and I started falling—I couldn't stop it.

The ushers caught me as I hit the floor, but I couldn't move. I was conscious, but I physically couldn't get up. I thought, I don't believe this. I don't believe this. I've fallen, and I can't get up. But there I was, covered in what I can only describe as a blanket of peace. After a minute or two, I felt that presence lift, and I sat up.

After that night, we had a decision to make. We could go back to the church that was in line with the denomination I had been a part of before, where things were familiar. Or we could come back to this place—where something had happened to us.

I'm so glad I let Ken eat that cake. And that I followed him to the church with "all the people." He led us straight into God's plan for our lives.

seven

DIVINE TURNAROUNDS

I have always thought it was interesting how people respond to the supernatural presence of God. Some experience the gifts of the Holy Spirit and the power of God, and they get scared, wanting to run the other direction. Others experience it and run toward God, saying, "Lord, I want more." Time would prove us to be the second of the two.

The next Sunday, I was quick to take the spiritual lead again. I told Tabatha, "Let's go back to that church we visited on Tuesday." I didn't know what denomination they were. I didn't know much about the place in general. All I knew was that I was touched by God there.

When we went back, it must have been right after 9/11 or very close to it. I remember so vividly—the pastor was talking about having faith in God and trusting Him in times of uncertainty. He spoke unlike any preacher I had ever heard before. There was a boldness and spiritual authority in his words that gripped my attention. It seemed as if he knew God personally, and he spoke about the Bible like it was truth.

He talked about how, after the 9/11 attacks, Satan would love for us to walk in fear. But as believers, we weren't called to be fearful—not of terrorism, not of anything. "God has not given us a spirit of fear," he said, "but of power, love, and a sound mind."

He sounded like a coach getting his team ready to win a championship. Like a general preparing his army for battle. The crowd was fired up, and for the first time, the Bible made sense to me. I remember getting my hands on that cassette tape and sharing it with all my family and friends. At that time, the nation was in mourning. People were afraid. The constant threats of more attacks left people crippled with fear. But I would pass out that tape and say, "You don't have to give in to fear. We are called to walk by faith and not by sight."

Looking back, I can see so clearly how God was ordering our steps. The things I had unknowingly prophesied, the correction I had received from people around me, even the timing of finding this church right after 9/11—it all lined up. I think God used it to tenderize my heart for what He wanted to do next.

Tabatha and I kept going back to that church. Again. And again. And again. By the fourth visit, we decided to make it our church home. That Sunday, they were having a corporate giving event called Super Sunday. That was the day we finally gave the $1,000 we had wanted to give a month earlier.

To this day, I don't know where that money came from. It was all we had. But I was falling in love with Jesus, and the Bible says, "Where your treasure is, there your heart will be also." By the end of that service, we had made up our minds. We were all in. And since we had just given away our life savings, we figured we might as well go ahead and join the church too.

I was so new to church. I remember being unsure of so many things, but I could see something happening in Ken that made me want to follow. In the beginning, he took my hand a lot—pulling me toward God. He took my hand and pulled me to the altar. He took my hand as we gave our first big offering. He took my hand as we joined this new church home. We didn't know it then, but every step we took toward God, together, was strengthening our marriage.

It was like getting shot out of a spiritual cannon. Within a matter of weeks, I had received the baptism of the

Holy Spirit, started praying in my prayer language, joined this new church, gave my first large offering, stopped drinking, stopped clubbing, and lost all desire to do ungodly things. I wasn't perfect. I had a lot of growing to do. But something had shifted. The Holy Spirit was changing me.

I was learning things at an accelerated rate. I mean, I was devouring the Word. I tend to be an all-or-nothing kind of girl, so when it came to growing closer to my Heavenly Father—the One who had been there all along, but I had just found out about—it was on like popcorn. I dove in headfirst, figuring I'd deal with the consequences later. I went to Bible studies, membership classes, discipleship courses, women's meetings—anything I could get to. I was discovering, for the first time, not just who God was but who I was.

I studied the Bible, I prayed, and I made faith declarations. And then something happened. I realized that if God is a healer, then He could probably heal me from depression. So, I asked God to heal me. I made it my first faith project. I was going to believe Him for my healing.

Back then, depression wasn't talked about like it is today. It wasn't considered a real illness by most people. It was this mysterious thing that made people sad. People thought you could just snap out of it. If only it were that simple. By that point, I had been battling depression for twelve years, and I was ready to be free. For the first time, someone had offered me a way out—Jesus.

Part of my healing from depression was forgiveness. Unforgiveness had been one of the major chains keeping me bound. I had bitterness and hatred toward people who had abused me as a child. Through prayer, God showed me how to forgive. In His presence, I became aware of my own sin—my own need for forgiveness. How could I hold others in contempt when I needed so much mercy and grace? I asked God to help me forgive, but at first, it didn't feel real. So, I prayed. And prayed. And prayed. Every day, I kept praying for my abuser. I imagined their face smiling with joy. I prayed for their health. I blessed their children.

For months, I prayed and believed God. But nothing changed. Until one morning… I woke up as usual. I got dressed and read my bible. Afterwards, I went downstairs. As I reached the bottom of the stairs, I felt something happening. I kept walking toward the living room, and with every step forward, it was as if something was lifting off me. I literally saw a shadow leave my body, hovering through the living room before exiting through the wall of my home. In that moment, I felt alive. I became spiritually alert. It was like I had been living in black and white, and suddenly, I could see in full color. I knew, without a doubt, that my healing had come. God had delivered me from depression. I had broken the chains through prayer, through forgiveness, through trusting God. I was free. I was healed. And I've stayed healed for over 23 years now.

Rebuilding What Was Broken

Many people try to fix their relationship without the right tools. That's hard—if not impossible—at times. It's like trying to dig a ditch without a shovel. The right tools make the job so much easier. Have you ever played cards before? We love playing cards in our house, but it's impossible to win if all the cards aren't in the deck. Many people start off their marriages without the right tools or the right number of cards, and they wonder why things don't work. They're just missing key ingredients.

With all my weaknesses and failures, I didn't feel like I deserved anything from God. But that's what grace is—favor you don't deserve. Hopefully, I've painted a clear enough picture of who I used to be, so you don't hate me now… lol… but instead, you can see His amazing grace surrounding our lives. Twenty-five years later, people come to us for marriage advice. They look to us like we're some kind of spiritual rock stars, but that's just not true. We're just two broken people who decided to put God first and position ourselves as recipients of His grace.

The thing about grace is that you don't have to be super smart or talented to receive it. You don't have to measure up to earn it. God gives it freely because of His love. And His grace is available to you, just like it has been for us.

I didn't do anything special to earn these tools. God gave them to me by grace. That's why we feel such a passion to pay them forward. We didn't earn them. These tools aren't just available for smart people or rich people or connected people. They're more so available for humble people—people who are willing to trade in their own plans for His.

Then you have to work the tools. Work them when you don't feel like it. Work them when they don't seem to be working. Work them as unto the Lord. But work them. God will not work the tools for you. He will give you His grace, but what you do with the tools is completely up to you.

Here are the tools God gave us to help save our marriage. They are available for everyone:

A relationship with Jesus (salvation)

Baptism of the Holy Spirit (power)

The Word of God (understanding, insight, and spiritual nourishment)

A church home (community & examples)

Mentorship (accountability & training)

These five tools were the first installment of what God gave us to help turn our marriage around. Each one played an important role in building a better marriage.

Once again, tools by themselves didn't fix our marriage, and they won't fix yours. We had to learn how to use the tools correctly to get the most benefit out of them. God gave them to us from the beginning, but now it was up to us to use them to rebuild what was broken.

Every Promise Has A Process

By this time, our marriage was better, but it still wasn't perfect. On a scale of 1 to 10, I'd say we had moved up to a six. That was much better than a three, but we were still young in our faith, young in marriage, and learning so many new things at once. Thankfully, our church had a once-a-month meeting for married couples called Communication Lab.

Every first Friday, we would go and simply learn how to be a husband and a wife. A lot of what I teach today, I learned in those sessions over twenty years ago.

Oh yes, we had a lot to work on. When I was healed of depression, for the first time, I was able to see the turmoil in our marriage. Sorry, Babe, but at this point, I would have rated it a three.

After depression, I was happy. I wanted to go out and enjoy life. But Ken wasn't convinced. For me, my whole life had just changed. But to Ken? Nothing had changed. I still looked like the same person. I noticed he blew me off a lot. He was short with me. Just plain rude. But I tell you the truth—I didn't care. I could see right past that hard exterior. I married Ken because he swept me off my feet. He is brilliant, amazing, wonderful. I knew that man was still in there.

When I put myself in his shoes, it was revealing. I had been living in my own world, weighed down by my own struggles. I hadn't noticed that my husband was barely holding on. Failed expectations. Financial pressures. Lack of intimacy. A deep need for honor. He was angry and shut off. In self-protect mode, afraid of being disappointed. And although I hated it, I understood why he was that way. I had been emotionally checked out for most of our marriage, and he was paying the price for it. I think he missed the fun-loving, nurturing woman he had married. He wanted his best friend back. He had married the girl of his dreams—what happened to her?

Well, she was back. But he didn't know it yet.

I resisted a little bit at first because this was all new to me. I was learning how to live a Spirit-led life instead of a flesh-dominated one. Every once in a while, my flesh would rise up and get the best of me. However, to my credit, long gone were the days of taking my ring off, talking to other women, or threatening divorce. All those things were out of my heart and mind.

Tabatha did a lot to make our marriage better after she got the right tools. I started off slow, but it didn't take me long to get with the program. She treated me like the man I was becoming, not like the man I had been or even the man I was in that moment. That made me want to be a better man.

I decided to show him the new and improved Mrs. Tabatha Claytor. And honestly? I had fun doing it.

First, I wanted to serve him. I started doing things that would make him feel cared for and respected in his home. I organized his closet, ironed all of his clothes, and put them on hangers so he could just walk in and pick what he wanted to wear. I started making him lunch and dinner every day. I ignored his bad attitude and snarky comments. Talk about turning the other cheek!

He would come home, see that I had dinner waiting for him, and say, I already ate. I would call him before he left work and say, Don't eat out, I'm making dinner. Then he would come home late and miss it anyway. So I started wrapping his plate in plastic wrap, writing his name on it with a little heart, and leaving it in the fridge. BAM—there it is! Eventually, he started eating the food. (Because let's be real—food is his weakness.)

Then, I made a move that I knew would work. If successful, it would win him for good. I invented Ken's Night. One night a week, I set aside time to pamper my king with manicures, pedicures, scalp massages, and body massages. Sometimes we'd have a candlelit dinner with his favorite foods. If there was a game on, I'd put a platter of snacks in front of the TV and rub his shoulders while we watched together.

And no Ken's Night was complete without sex. Yes, my secret weapon. The first time I tried it, I came downstairs in my slinky outfit, perfume, hair done, makeup flawless. But he brushed me off like lint on a coat. I don't even think he looked at me.

I was humiliated. I even shed a few tears, but I prayed and asked God to help me be strong. (Plus, I'm from the hood—I know how to bounce back.)

So, the next day, I put on the same outfit and did it again.

This time, he couldn't resist.

That was the beginning of Ken's Night. And through those nights, we became friends again. We became lovers again.

Oh, the power of a praying wife.

She was very in tune to "taking care of her man." She treated me like royalty. And it was contagious. Now, I know that some of you might be thinking, that's just too much, or better yet, well, what did you do, Ken? If that's your question, I think you're missing the point. It wasn't about what I did or didn't do. It was about the power God gave her to win our marriage, no matter how I was acting.

After becoming so acquainted with the power of forgiveness during my healing process, I had no problem forgiving Ken for all of his shenanigans (lol). Who was I to hold his past against him? I didn't want him to hold my past against me. I wanted him to forgive me for all of the drama and pain I caused. Forgive me for all of the nights he felt alone—even though I was in bed right next to him. Forgive me for not noticing his needs. In my new walk with God, I was so thankful to be forgiven. I just wanted to give that same gift to my husband and anyone else who needed it. It was my pleasure to humble myself for the sake of my marriage and the man I vowed to love.

Too many people say, "I'll treat him better if he treats me better." Or, "If my wife did all those things for me, then I would do nice things for her." That's not how it works. People want a harvest without first sowing a seed. I'm not sharing these stories for you to judge my lack of production—I'm sharing them so you can see what happens when a faith-filled woman or man shifts their attention away from what their spouse is not doing and, instead, does what they do as unto the Lord. 1 Peter 3:1 (Amplified) says: "In the same way, you wives, be submissive to your own husbands [subordinate, not as inferior, but out of respect for the responsibilities entrusted to husbands and their accountability to God, and so partnering with them] so that even if some do not obey the word [of God], they may be won over [to Christ] without discussion by the godly lives of their wives."

She treated me like royalty from a pure heart. And my automatic response was to treat her like royalty in return. Sometimes, I messed up. But when I did, I knew it. I would have to come back and apologize. Sweetheart, I'm sorry.

When I was in the flesh, I knew it now. And because her stance was so holy, so faith-filled, and so pure, even if I acted wrong, I couldn't stay wrong. I soon felt conviction and knew I needed to make things right.

The principle that was at work was selflessness. We call it the Out-Bless Your Spouse Challenge. That's when one spouse does everything they can to out-bless the other, and the other spouse does the same. You take the attention off of what you're getting out of the relationship and, instead, focus on what you're giving to your spouse. The returns? Incredible. Two selfless people, walking in the agape love of God, looking to do good for one another.

That's when our marriage went from good to great. That's when we went from a 6 (or a 3 if you ask her, lol) on a scale of 1–10 to always hovering between 8 and 10. We loved being together again. It felt like the Butterfly Love days, but with maturity and stability. We became best friends again. We enjoyed each other again. We couldn't wait to spend time together at the end of each day. Sex? It was a pleasure. We set ourselves to learn each other. Learn to please each other. Meet each other's needs—emotionally, spiritually, and sexually.

And amazingly enough, as we started getting our marriage in line, our finances started getting in line, too. It was so surreal. It reminds me of the scripture that says when a husband and wife are in disagreement, their prayers are hindered (1 Peter 3:7). I didn't know it at the time, but those first two years of our marriage had closed God's ears to some of my prayers. But once I started loving His daughter and treating her the way I was supposed to, He opened the floodgates.

One of my greatest pleasures was watching my husband transform from spiritual childhood to spiritual manhood. I watched him shift from chasing fortune and status to chasing God. I watched him fall in love with Jesus. I would go to work and come home, and he'd still be in the same room, praying and fasting before the Lord. I'd have to check on him to make sure he was still alive and on planet Earth.

He started evangelizing, telling everyone who would listen about Jesus. One by one, friends, family—even clients—were getting saved. I watched him build our real estate business by faith. God blessed us, and we became prosperous. He started giving—paying for youth trips, paying off people's debts, blessing strangers, praying for people at dinner tables. I watched him step into his calling.

And when he said yes to God? It was full speed ahead.

And I was completely on board for the ride.

part three
A LOVE THAT ENDURES

eight
THE CALL

We were rocking and rolling, eating the good of the land. Ken was winning Realtor of the Year awards and multimillion-dollar sales awards. I was selling houses and becoming one of the top salespeople in my region. We went vacationing in Exuma, where we took an excursion to our own private island—THE BEST! We walked around like Adam and Eve in the garden (naked). We took ski trips to Tahoe, hitting the slopes all day and warming by the fire at night. We had parties, dinners, and barbecues for every occasion. It was Ken and Tabatha's world, and we were loving it.

But, we began to feel like God wanted us to do more. Up to this point, we believed we were called to finance the Kingdom. We were fine with being business owners because, for us, the deeper purpose of making money was to build God's Kingdom on earth. It was our dream to help pay for churches and orphanages. But we felt a pulling to do something more, to go deeper in our understanding of God and Scripture. So, we enrolled in a three-year Bible Institute designed to help us understand the Bible and discover our ministry calling. During that time, we both received a call to pastor and plant a church. We felt God transitioning us for a change.

At the time, I was working for a new home developer. It was an all-commission job, but it was lucrative. The few years I was there, I learned to use my faith even in the workplace. Yes, I worked hard, but I also believed God for my communities to sell out. And they did. It seemed silly for me to quit something so rewarding, but I knew I had to follow God's leading. I decided to resign from sales to open a real estate brokerage with Ken. I wanted to support his dream, so I made his dream our dream, and we did it. We opened our real estate office, and it was a success.

Then, we got pregnant! We swayed back and forth about when to have children. I would be ready, and he wouldn't. Then he would be ready, and I wouldn't. Finally, we both agreed—it was time. We thought I'd get pregnant right away, but it took a few months. Just when we were beginning to get discouraged, Ken came home with a book called

Supernatural Childbirth. I was in the kitchen making dinner when Ken came in like he had just won the lottery. He threw his briefcase on the table and started digging inside of it. Out came this small pink book. Having already read it, he began to tell me the entire book in ten minutes. I was a believer! Then he put his hands on my womb and prayed for me.

Of course, I picked up that book like it was a roast beef sandwich and devoured it. It was filled with Scriptures about God's promise for us to be able to have children and testimonies of women who overcame the worst odds and gave birth. It had never occurred to us to go to the Bible about our pregnancy concerns. But now we knew—take everything to God in prayer! Within a couple of weeks, I tested positive. We were about to have a baby girl.

In 2005, I began to wrestle with our future. A peer in real estate asked me what I was going to do in business next. For some reason, I felt unsure. I loved business but was feeling a call into ministry. Instead of staying in a place of uncertainty, I decided to fast, pray, and seek God concerning our callings and next steps in business and life.

I set aside 40 days to fast, pray, and seek God for direction. Not all-day fasts or water-only fasts, but I switched between 6:00 am–6:00 pm fasts, fruit and vegetable fasts, and Daniel fasts, depending on the week. Right in the middle of the fast, around day 20, I was watching Christian television. A program came on with a preacher who had a church in Florida. I had always had a natural desire to live in Florida. I never really thought much about it, but it always seemed like a great place to live.

Coming from West Virginia, Florida seemed like a world away. When my family went on vacation, we would go to Virginia Beach or maybe Myrtle Beach, South Carolina. Anything south of that seemed too far. I had only been to Florida three times as a child that I could remember—once to Disney World at six years old, once when I was ten years old for the Jr. Olympics in Gainesville, where I placed sixth in the nation in the long jump, and once to Orlando when I was fourteen years old.

Fast forward 16 years (past middle school, high school, college, a bad marriage, meeting God, a good marriage). I was sitting in my living room, watching a preacher in Florida on TV, in the middle of fasting and praying about our next move. I knew I was called to pastor, and I was in my second year of Bible school, but I didn't know when or where. During a commercial break, as I was walking toward the bathroom, I asked God under my breath, "God, if you've called us to Florida, where would it be?" Immediately, I heard the Lord say, "Gainesville."

I said, "Say that again"... and He repeated, "Gainesville."

I knew by the way He answered, it wasn't Gainesville, Georgia, or Gainesville, Virginia. It was Gainesville, *Florida.*

THE CALL

This was a huge moment for Tabatha and I. We knew no one in Gainesville at the time. We had no connections there. But I knew this was a God moment. It was the clearest I had ever heard Him. The next thing I did was tell Tabatha.

By this time, I knew that if Ken said it, it was probably true. The Lord was with my husband, and I knew it. I remember the day God spoke Gainesville to him. I was pregnant and in the kitchen chopping veggies. He was watching TV and suddenly jumped up from the couch like a man on a mission. He marched through the kitchen to his office, tossing papers around like he was in deep conversation with someone, but no one was there. I could feel in my spirit that something was happening.

Later, he came out of his office and told me that we were moving to Florida to start a church. I said, "Baby, if God said it, we can do it. I'm all in."

We agreed that if this was God, we would tell our pastor and see what he said. My pastor knew I was called to pastor probably before I did. By this time, I wasn't just serving in the church—I was an armor bearer and even on the board of directors. He had been training me for this moment for years, whether I knew it or not.

Pastors hate to see people go. Even when we pray for you and bless you, there's a part of us that wants to keep the band together. That's human and natural. It's like with your kids—when they say they want to move across the country, you're like, Nooo… why? But at the end of the day, you want them to follow their callings and destinies. Pastoring is very similar to parenting. Any good pastor loves extremely hard.

I wanted to meet with my pastor—not just to tell him we were leaving but to get his blessing and covering for what we were doing. I needed his coaching. I needed his guidance. I needed his pastoring now more than ever. The meeting went extremely well. He agreed that we were called to Gainesville and gave us his full blessing. He only asked us to do one thing—"Don't tell anyone else for now. Let's keep this between us for the time being, and I will let others know at the right time."

Oops. Out of excitement, I had already told a couple of people. But from that day forward, we didn't say a word to anyone unless we ran it by him first. And that was a good thing—because the Lord told us that we wouldn't start until 2007. We had 1.5 to 2 years to wait.

But wait! Those years flew by because we had our first child, Hannah Nicole, in May of 2005. It was Sunday morning before church. I was in the pantry, leaning down to pick up a box of cereal. When I stood up, I felt my water break. Only, it wasn't a dramatic movie moment with water gushing everywhere—it was just a little bit, so I wasn't even sure if my water had broken or if I had just peed my pants. (I mean, seriously, my belly was huge.)

THE CALL

I called my doctor, and she assured me everything was normal. She said it was probably the beginning of labor and advised me to take a walk and monitor the contractions. Now, Ken was scheduled to serve that morning, so I told him to go ahead and go but to keep his phone on because if I needed him, I'd call.

He went to church. He came home. Still no contractions. Finally, later that night, we went to the hospital. I was believing for a supernatural childbirth. I read the book. I had the faith. I declared that my labor would be pain-free, no epidural, no episiotomy, no complications. Long story short: I had pain, I had an epidural, and I had an episiotomy. I had everything.

My water broke, but I never went into labor, even after walking miles around my neighborhood. So I had to be induced. And let me tell you—if natural labor is a slow burn, induced labor is like being thrown into a fire pit. I had the exact opposite of no pain. The farthest you could get from no pain, that's what I had. I felt everything. I was shaking, throwing up, and dealing with diarrhea—sometimes all at the same time.

At that point, all human decency was gone. My husband was seeing me in ways he never imagined. As much as I didn't want him to witness me in that state, I needed him by my side. And to my surprise, he turned into a teddy bear. He was so gentle and so calm. I just wanted to love him. Twenty-four hours later, our baby girl was born. Eight pounds, three ounces. Yes, I said twenty-four hours. The struggle was real.

The next few months were hard for me. This was the first time I had really used my faith for something, and what I believed for didn't come to pass. I was crushed. Physically, I felt like I had been run over by a herd of elephants. Emotionally, I was grateful to have my baby, but hormonally, I was everywhere. I had to lean on God and other moms who had been through it before.

There were so many things I wasn't prepared for. The pregnancy books didn't tell me how sore my nipples would be, how exhausted I would feel, or how big and squishy my body would be postpartum.

One day, I had a moment. I had been up all night with the baby. I was hungry. I was sore. I was sitting in my rocker, nursing the baby, when Ken walked in—fresh, clean, and well-rested. His clothes didn't have baby drool on them. He hadn't been up all night. He was living his best life, and suddenly, I wanted to punch him in the face.

I mean, I really wanted to fight him.

For a split second, I was furious. Why does he get to have all the fun? I carried this baby for nine months and that was the easy part?!

It wasn't my finest moment. But somehow, I think Ken felt the imaginary punches I was throwing at him because, a couple of hours later, a friend (who was also a pediatrician) showed up at the house to help me through it. Thank God for friends. And thank you, babe, for loving me through it.

No, my birthing plan didn't go exactly as I had believed. But then again—yes, it did. I was right to plan and believe. But I was wrong to feel condemned, mad at God, Ken, or myself when things didn't go as expected. We make plans, but God directs our paths. As long as God is directing, I'm here for the ride. He always leads us to safety. And in the end, I had a healthy baby and a healthy mom. What else matters?

We never wanted to be the went. We always wanted to be the sent. Too many people receive a call from God, but they step out in the wrong way or in the wrong timing. Getting our pastor's full blessing was a top priority for Tabatha and me.

We weren't starting a church because we were offended, wanted to do something new, or didn't like something at our old church. We actually loved our church. We didn't want to leave. We served there. We preached there. I was on the board of directors. I was part of the teaching team—one of the few people trusted to preach when our pastor was away. All of our friends were there. Our community was there.

Not to mention, we were at the top of our business cycle. Long gone were the days of financial struggles. We were living in a 6,500-square-foot home with a movie theater, fitness center, and even a chef, maid, and nanny.

And we were only a family of three at the time. We were living the dream.

But God had a different dream for us.

Yeah, we loved our lives in the D.C. area. Our favorite restaurants and parks, family and friends, our businesses. We had built a beautiful life. But we believed that whatever we gave up for the sake of the Gospel, God would restore. We knew that if God was calling us to Gainesville, that meant there were new family and friends we hadn't met yet—people waiting for us to show up.

Gainesville wasn't an escape for us. We weren't leaving something bad to go find something good. We were leaving a church we loved and a city we loved to move to a place where we knew no one.

It reminds me of the story of the rich young ruler. Jesus told him, "Sell all you have, give to the poor, and follow me." The Bible says the young man walked away sad because he had great possessions. Thankfully, we did the opposite of that story. We sold all we had, left everything we knew, and moved to Gainesville toward the end of 2006.

Those 1.5 to 2 years were challenging. Knowing we were leaving but not being able to tell people yet was hard. Continuing to serve and do business, knowing we were about to leave it all behind, was hard. Putting our house on the market without explaining why was hard. But that training was necessary.

Starting a church is not for the faint of heart. You have to be tough.

That year, we had a big Thanksgiving dinner. While everyone was feasting, I remember looking around and cherishing the moment. We were leaving in two months. This was our last big gathering before we moved to Florida. I was a bit emotional, but I couldn't tell anyone.

We wanted to be obedient to our instruction and preparation for ministry. So, we sucked it up and did what we had to do—but it was hard. We had to navigate how to prepare our businesses, clients, and families for the transition without telling them we were moving into ministry.

And Florida was so far away!

It could have been a stressful time for us, but we would not allow it. We were on assignment, and we could not wait to start what God had put in our hearts.

Big Transitions

A couple of weeks before the move, our pastors finally told the congregation that Tabatha and I would be moving to Gainesville, Florida, to start a church. After 14 years of ministry, we were the first couple they had ever sent out to plant a church with their full blessing. That was a big deal to us. We just wanted to make them proud and steward what God had given us well. There was a mix of emotions, I'm sure. Most people were excited and wished us well, but

I know some close to us felt blindsided. "Why didn't you tell us?" they wondered.

It didn't make it easier that decisions like this require bold obedience. It's almost like leaving one life to build another. It's not about cutting people off, but the sacrifice is so great that things just won't be the same. Some of that cost we foresaw, and some we had no idea was coming.

Leaving the house was surreal. The furniture was all packed and on its way to Florida to meet us there. I looked into Hannah's nursery one last time. The walls were still painted pink, with bows and hearts bordering the top. I stood in the foyer, remembering the Christmas party where we lined the staircase and sang carols. Even now, I can still hear the sound of Hannah's little feet running down the hallway, full speed, to greet whoever was at the door. Those moments are etched in my memory.

We took one last trip to the car. Car seat, check. Diaper bag, check. Suitcases, check. The three of us—Ken, Hannah, and I—stood in the foyer, holding hands. We said a quick prayer, and then Ken looked at me and asked, "Are you ready?" But the question meant more than just, "Are you ready to get in the car?" It was really asking, "Are you ready to close this chapter and begin a new one? Are you ready to start over? To trust God? To fight?" I looked him in the eyes and spoke back, "I'm ready." We sealed it with a kiss and closed the door behind us.

THE CALL

We left for Florida just a few days before my 31st birthday in January 2007. When we boarded that plane, it was just the three of us—our little family—with nothing but a vision from God and faith in our hearts.

The transition from Washington, D.C. to Gainesville was not easy. We had to find everything new—new dry cleaners, new grocery stores, new barbers, new doctors. The culture was completely different. For us, it felt like moving to the mission field. The style of dress, the lingo, the weather—nothing was the same. Gainesville and Washington, D.C., had almost nothing in common. But we knew we were called to love people and build a church where lives would be changed. That's exactly what we planned to do.

Moving from D.C. to Florida was a complete culture shock. In D.C., we wore suits, white collars, and ties. In Gainesville, people wore cutoff shorts and flip-flops. I shopped at Whole Foods in D.C., but in Gainesville, there were no organic grocery stores. And basements? There are no basements in Florida! But we embraced the change. We bought a house with a pool, fired up the grill, and ate barbecue while swimming in January. We were living the life.

Our church launched on April 8, 2007, right in the middle of a recession. These days, I hear about churches launching with 100, 200, or even 500 people. Some raise $200,000 to $500,000 before they even open their doors. That wasn't our story. Our sending church gave us $20,000

and paid for our audio equipment, which was a huge blessing. As for our launch team? We had about six adults and three kids. That was it. But oh, don't forget—we had one big God.

We didn't feel like we were behind the curve. We weren't smart enough to study demographics or assemble things more strategically. At the time, we had childlike faith. God said, "Gainesville," and we said, "Yes." It was His job to provide the rest.

Don't get me wrong—I wish I had known more. It would have saved us a lot of pain. I'm so impressed with young pastors today who study the area, build large launch teams, and secure donors to back their vision. I applaud them. I wish I had known half of what they know now, back then. But honestly, if we had waited for everything to line up perfectly, we might never have left. Sometimes, we get so caught up in hitting certain markers that we won't move until it's safe. That wasn't us. That's never been our story. We've always been called to walk by faith—taking a step, trusting God to give us more on the way.

We definitely did things the hard way, but I have no regrets. It made us who we are. We started by having Bible studies in our home. I'd cook a big dinner, and Ken would deliver a big message. It was some of the sweetest fellowship. Ken would even bring strangers home for Bible study! One of the first members of our church was our lawn care guy. He had a heart for ministry, so he would go out and minister to the homeless and bring them home. He'd introduce them to me, and we'd give them clothes from our closet, shoes, suitcases—whatever we had. We just wanted to show people the love of Jesus.

I never wanted to go back to the way things were in the first two years of our marriage, and thankfully, our relationship never did. As you'll see, there were other battles we had to fight, but a struggling marriage was not one of them. So, when I say, "Hard times are here again," I'm talking about finances.

When we started our church in Gainesville, we had some seed money from our sending church, which was a blessing. But it wasn't enough to cover all the demands of ministry. Today, I tell people it takes $200,000 to $300,000 to launch a church effectively. We put in another $25,000 of our own personal money, and for almost the entire first year, neither Tabatha nor I took a salary. We lived off the savings from our real estate business. But after about a year, our savings—six figures' worth—was completely gone. Financially, we were back to where we were when we first met.

This was another really hard season for us. The real estate market crashed between 2007 and 2008. We'd hired a manager to run our business in D.C. while we planted the church in Gainesville, but unfortunately, the person we hired tried to do a hostile takeover and push us out. We had to shut it down, which cost us thousands of dollars. At the same time, we had bought a new house in Gainesville—smaller than our last one, but still in a new community. We were the first new home built there, and when the market crashed in 2008, so did our home's value. No other new homes were built for years. We even tried selling it for $150,000 less than we paid, but no one was buying.

Things got so bad financially that we had to send Tabatha back to work. Now, when I say we had to send Tabatha back to work, I want to be clear—my wife has always been an incredible helpmate. From the very beginning, she has willingly set aside her own career goals and desires to help me pursue mine. Actually, let me correct that—she didn't give up her dreams for mine. She sacrificed for our team to win. Team Claytor.

It's true. I've always been a team player. I remember back when I first got into real estate, it was for the "team" and out of obedience to God. I was young in my faith, but I knew I heard His voice. At the time, Ken's real estate sales were taking off, and he needed an assistant to help him manage everything. I was preparing to leave my job as an HR assistant for something more meaningful. An art teacher position had opened at a local high school, and I was excited about it.

But the day before my interview, God spoke to me during my morning run. I heard Him clearly: "Don't go to the interview. Don't take the job. Work for Ken. Help him build this business because this will be the foundation for your family to grow." I began to cry. I was disappointed because I felt like I was giving up my dream. I wanted to give back. I wanted to make a difference. But how was I supposed to do that by selling houses?

Yet, I knew what I heard. And God wasn't done speaking.

"Don't worry," He said. "One day, you'll teach my kids."

At the time, I didn't understand the weight of those words. But now, looking back, I see it all so clearly. So, when I needed to go back to work, it was easy. We were on a kingdom assignment and whatever I needed to do to push the vision, I was there for it.

When two become one, it's no longer about individual success. It's about what the team needs in a given season. When I win, we win. When she wins, we win. Too many couples focus on their personal aspirations without considering the collective whole.

Tabatha is one of the most innovative, creative, and intelligent people I know. She is a natural builder. She's not the type of leader who micro-manages people, but if you give her a vision, she will execute it flawlessly. She will research, watch YouTube tutorials, attend conferences, and then turn around and build something incredible. She has that gift.

So here we were—new city, new church, no money. We made the decision that I would start receiving a small salary from the church while she went back to work. By this point, she had already climbed the corporate ladder, made six figures, helped me build a real estate business, and started a church in a new city. But due to the market crash, the only job she could find was in Ocala, Florida—about a 40-minute drive from Gainesville—as an assistant to a real estate broker. For the sake of "Team Claytor," she took the job, making a whopping $35,000 a year.

And then... she got fired.

Looking back, I should have just started the daycare from the beginning and skipped the whole job thing. I was way overqualified for that position. They tried to create a hybrid role for me, but it just didn't work out. So, after ninety days, I was let go.

I had never been fired before. But there I was—fired. Yet, I wasn't angry. I wasn't upset at God. That's just not our approach to hardship. We believe that all things work together for good (Romans 8:28). Instead of despair, I actually thought, *okay, devil, we're about to show you something.*

Ken and I both felt relief, too. That 40-minute commute was brutal. Plus, we were still paying someone in D.C. $50,000 a year to manage the last of our real estate business there, which was more than I was making at the time. Everything felt upside down. It was one of those moments where we just had to trust that God was working behind the scenes.

Instead of looking for another job, we asked ourselves, "What can we do that aligns with the vision of the church?" That's when the idea for Faith Academy was born.

Neither of us had ever run a daycare before, but we saw a need. We could offer a Christian daycare for our church and the community. It would provide jobs for teachers and childcare workers, and it would bring families into the church. Most importantly, it would give Tabatha the opportunity to build something meaningful instead of taking another job that didn't fit her.

So, we figured it out.

We built that daycare fast. Yes, I had business experience, but I also had God's favor. One thing about us is that we are not afraid to try something new. And we are definitely not afraid to fail.

Any successful person will tell you that failure is not really failure—it's just a learning opportunity. The only time you truly fail is when you quit, and momma ain't raise no quitters! So we did what we always do: we figured it out.

The daycare started with just one child—our daughter, Hannah. But we grew it to over 100 kids. It was an essential part of our ministry for several years. It provided jobs, helped us financially, and served our community in a huge way.

Eventually, I hired someone to take over my role at the daycare. I remember my last day so vividly. I was still hanging around, helping out here and there, but I was six months pregnant with our second baby.

Ken came looking for me. He opened the classroom door just as I was trying to shimmy myself off the floor. I had been sitting down, working on a project, and I guess I had been there too long because my legs didn't want to cooperate. I must have looked a mess because Ken took one look at me and said, "You're done."

At first, I pushed back—because I like to work. But I remember, about a week later, sitting at home with my three-year-old, propping my feet up, thinking, *Thank you, Jesus. I needed this.*

Meanwhile, the church was growing fast! People were being healed. Marriages were being restored. Thousands were coming to know Jesus. By the time we hit year five, we had two locations in Gainesville, and we were holding services at the Dr. Phillips Center for Performing Arts on the campus of the University of Florida. It was an 1,800-seat auditorium, and no church had ever held regular Sunday services there until we did.

It was a season of excitement. Anticipation. Growth. But while everything looked good on the outside, inside, we were experiencing incredible pain.

Every Call Has A Cost

The first five years of ministry were both challenging and rewarding. We were learning how to be lead pastors, and God was adding people to our church consistently. Even though we had about a thousand people attending and multiple locations, I kept feeling like something wasn't quite right. The vision God had given me wasn't what I was seeing. Our church was doing amazing things, but we weren't reaching different ethnicities as well as I had hoped, and it felt like we weren't as missional as we needed to be.

I was taught not to reinvent the wheel, so many of the systems, language, and structures we used were simply copied and pasted from my previous church experiences. Over time, I realized that what works in one context doesn't always work in another. What works for one pastor might be the downfall of another. In retrospect, I now understand that the great foundation I had been given was actually *hindering* something inside me. I was so faithful to another man's vision that I hadn't fully walked into my own.

I didn't have the words to explain it then, but now I recognize that I was experiencing what I call wearing Saul's armor. In Scripture, when David was about to fight Goliath, King Saul gave him his own armor—something of great honor. But David quickly realized that, while it worked for Saul, it didn't fit him. He would have been weighed down, unable to move effectively. So instead, David picked up his own weapon—a simple slingshot and five smooth stones—and fought his *way*. That was the season I was in. If I was going to defeat the giant in front of me, I had to come into my own identity as a leader.

That transition was not easy for me, our church, or my marriage. During this time, the Lord led me to study the five fastest-growing and most influential churches in America. For two years, I studied their systems—how they communicated, how they assimilated people, and how they managed their affairs. God began downloading insights to me about building a church that could reach people of all backgrounds while remaining filled with the power of the Holy Spirit.

So, I made the decision to shift the way we did church—not for convenience, but to reach more people and transform more lives. I thought our congregation would celebrate this move toward our new vision. But I quickly learned something about leadership—some people are married to their interpretation of the vision more than the vision itself. I also learned that some people will call you *Pastor* but are not actually ready to be led.

It reminded me of the Israelites in the wilderness. God had called them to the Promised Land and gave them an anointed leader in Moses. Yet, once they faced hardship, they wanted to go back to Egypt. The comfort of the past spoke louder to them than the glory of what could be.

THE CALL

Five years in, our church was growing, and so was our family. In 2011, we gave birth to our third child. At that point, we already had two beautiful girls, Hannah and Charity. The years had flown by so fast that we almost forgot to have another baby! So, we got pregnant right away with Charity. Hannah was four when Charity was born. Then, just nine months later, when I was down to my last five pounds of baby weight, I got pregnant again!

This time, we really wanted a boy, and the whole church was excited along with us. On a Sunday morning, we revealed the gender results. As the moment approached, I started acting nervous, dabbing my forehead with a pink napkin. The entire congregation deflated—they thought it was another girl! But then, we revealed, It's a boy! and the whole church erupted in celebration. It was such a fun moment.

Ken and I were growing in every way—our family, our personal journeys, and our ministry. But the changes happening inside of us weren't just natural growth; they were God-ordained. He was pruning, perfecting, and preparing us for something we had never seen before. There was an expression of faith unique to us that God wanted to release.

At first, we were so new to the church world that we had no idea what that expression would look like. We just started building. But over those first several years, God developed our identity as leaders—our sound, our structure, and our vision. Suddenly, church on Sunday wasn't enough.

We wanted more. We became intoxicated with vision. Not because what we had built was bad, but because God was doing a new thing in us.

The manna we had survived on in the wilderness was running out. It was time to step into the Promised Land.

The changes we made to our church—including the name change to Alive Church—weren't about doing what I wanted. Truth is, I liked what we had. But I loved the people we were called to reach more.

Rather than building a church that religious people would love, I started asking, How can we build a church that unreligious people would actually attend—and be transformed, not turned off? How could we build a church where disciples could be made regardless of race, ethnicity, or political persuasion. Those are different lenses to look through when building church. Thus, it became more important to me to build a church to reach more people than to build a church that I liked. Tabatha and I have been through a lot. But this might have been the worst.

It was bad for me because it was bad for Ken. I've always been the type to ignore negativity. Growing up in the projects, I learned early that people can be crazy—so why should I let crazy people's opinions dictate my emotions? Some people can be brilliant in one area and completely clueless in another. I once knew a nurse who could run an entire medical unit but would still leave for cigarette breaks every few hours. My husband is brilliant in a lot of things, but I draw the line when

THE CALL

he comes in the kitchen telling me how to cook. Smart in one area, not so much in another.

During this five-to-six-year period, I took a lot of lashes. Betrayal, false accusations, abandonment, and rejection—all from people we had prayed for, mentored, and loved deeply. One person in our leadership team looked me in the eye and said, "I don't like Alive Church."

That was devastating.

This was someone in leadership telling me to my face that they weren't with me, didn't want to be here, and didn't support where we were going. When you are obeying God, and just trying to build something that will glorify Him, those words are like daggers to the heart of the pastor. This person was at least bold enough to tell me to my face, but there were others that we loved on, prayed for, ordained, and gave our lives to for a decade that just vanished. They spoke volumes though they didn't speak a word. The message was clear: We don't like you. We don't agree with where you're taking this church.

I was shocked at how Christians could be so judgy and ungodly. In hindsight, I almost want to go back and tell all of them to leave my husband alone with their crazy, mean selves. I'm a little disappointed that I didn't go hood on them. Then they would have something to talk about (lol). All jokes aside, I had compassion for those people. I had grace for the moment. I would bless the people and let them go to another church or whatever they wanted to do. As for Ken and me, we were going to keep serving God. I think it can be confusing for church leaders to understand that we serve God first and then His people. I will say this though; those disgruntled Christians were few compared to the thousands of kind, loving Christians that I know and have known over the years.

That was my darkest moment. More than the financial struggles we had endured. More than the unfaithfulness to my wife in my younger years—those were youthful lusts I grew out of. The financial challenges? I knew we could figure those out. But this… this was deeper. This was an assassination on my character. It was an attack on who I was as a person. It wasn't just rejection—it was a rejection of my leadership and my calling.

People love to say, "It's not personal." Maybe for them it's not. But for me? How could it not be personal? I was the one who left everything—who moved to a city where I didn't know a single person, just because God said go. I was the one who opened my home for Bible studies, who welcomed homeless people into my house—while my two-year-old daughter was still there. I was the one who sold my car to give in a special offering, then had to drive the church van for a season or just ask for rides home.

This was extremely personal to me. And if it wasn't, I would be no good as a pastor. Unfortunately, not everyone sees it that way. Some people treat their leaders with contempt, with suspicion, as if we're just money-hungry preachers looking to fill our own bellies. But I know the truth. I know the countless pastors who have given everything to serve God's people—who have sacrificed, wept, and labored in love to care for the flock entrusted to them.

I won't go into all the details. But I will say this: it hurt. I was never diagnosed with depression. I never went to a doctor or sought help. But looking back, this—this season right here—was the darkest moment of my life.

Ken was struggling. At first, he handled it well, but over time, it started wearing on him. He became withdrawn—not quitting, but no longer enjoying life. He kept preaching, kept leading, but I could tell the light inside him was dimming.

I knew better than to push him. He had been working nonstop for about a decade. He needed a break. So, I just made sure I was there—his biggest cheerleader, his quiet strength.

What's funny is, I never stopped preaching. I never stopped leading the church. I never stopped being a father to my kids or a husband to my wife. But the light was off. The joy was gone. I almost hated coming to church—it had become a place of pain instead of the place of purpose I once envisioned. This wasn't what I signed up for. This wasn't what I imagined when I said *yes* to God.

That was the season when Tabatha stepped in the most. She carried the weight that I couldn't. She led when I felt lost. Thank God for strong women—women who lead in the church, in the home, and in the unseen battles. Slowly but surely, I began to turn things around. But I had to turn things around in my heart and mind before I could turn things around in the church. Because real change doesn't happen around you until it happens in you.

I'll always be grateful for the people who stood with us through those lean years—the ones who trusted my leadership even when they couldn't see where we were going. The ones who prayed for me, for my family, and for those who had gotten lost in the wilderness of their own confusion. God saw your faithfulness. He saw your labor of love. And I hope now, after all these years, you see the fruit of what we built together.

In that season, I needed a strong wife. I needed her encouragement. I needed her support. I needed her to pick me up when I was down. Too many husbands and wives watch their spouse go through a dark season and, instead of lifting them up, they kick them while they're already struggling. They check out. They walk away. They abandon ship just like everyone else. Don't do that.

Be a hero in the home when you are needed the most.

That season tested everything we had built. But it also prepared us. It refined us. Strengthened us. And we came out better for it. Because what the enemy meant for evil, God was already turning for good.

It Was All Worth It

I was ready for the moment. I had spent years at home with the kids, and while I loved them dearly, I was craving something that challenged my mind—something that reminded me I was more than just a mom. When I stepped into the office, it didn't take long to see why Ken had been struggling so much. We had a lot of work to do.

Nothing was illegal or ungodly, but it was far from excellent. The office was being run more like a small, family-owned business than the thriving nonprofit organization we knew it could be. There was little structure, policies were weak, and accountability was almost nonexistent. If we were going to grow, we had to do better. So, we got to work. We had to make tough decisions—firing people, hiring the right ones, cutting budgets, and retraining staff. It was difficult, but it felt familiar. It reminded me of the early days when I first started working with Ken, helping him build the infrastructure of his real estate business from the ground up.

Slowly, we established a culture of excellence. We implemented clear policies, created thorough handbooks, and developed systems that held people accountable. It wasn't easy, but looking back, I would do it again and again. Because this—this season of hard work and restructuring—was the foundation of what we see today. A thriving, well-run church that not only preaches the Gospel but also supports spiritual, emotional, and basic human needs around the world.

We're still not where we want to be, but thank God, we're not where we used to be. And that is something to be proud of.

Slowly but surely, we began to turn things around. When we first started casting new vision, I naively thought it would happen overnight, that one big adjustment would shift everything into place. I didn't realize it would take five to six years of small, incremental changes, each one building upon the last. Looking back, I now see the protection and grace of God in that slow, steady transformation.

I am grateful for that dark season. As painful as it was, it deepened my perspective and strengthened my anointing. I've always heard that it's the crushing of the grapes that produces the wine, the pressing of the olives that brings forth the oil. That season was my crushing, my pressing. And now, standing on the other side, I see the fruit.

Most people today would agree that there is something special about our church—a unique culture, a powerful anointing, a presence that cannot be manufactured. I would say, "to God be the glory," but I also know that every call comes with a cost. And if I had to do it all over again to produce the fruit we see now, I would. Without hesitation.

nine
MIRACLES IN THE MESS

I felt really good about where we had come from as a church. Our church was finally becoming what I had always envisioned—*as it is in heaven* (which I later wrote about in my book on racial reconciliation and unity). It was amazing to see. White people, Black people, Brown people, Yellow people, and everyone in between calling Alive Church home. It was beautiful to witness the impact we were making globally as well. As we began investing 10% of all our revenue back into missions, we saw lives transformed in South Africa, India, and beyond. All because we were willing to make some much-needed adjustments to how we did church.

Believe it or not, I started to love church again. Some people didn't like our style of music, but I enjoyed it. Everything we did, I fully embraced. If I didn't enjoy it, I recognized it as Saul's armor—I cut it off and did it our way. Not as a dismissal of the past, but out of respect for our authenticity. The people God started sending to our church were different too. We liked the same things, we saw the world in a similar way, and that was refreshing. It was proof that authenticity and context are huge factors in healthy, fruitful ministry.

But deep in my heart, I heard the Lord say, "It's time to expand." For years, I believed we would have multiple campuses in multiple cities. My plan had always been to stay in Gainesville and send out campus pastors to plant in other cities. The city I had been praying about for years was Jacksonville, Florida. But something strange happened—I started to sense that I wasn't supposed to send someone else. I was supposed to send myself again.

The devil is a liar! I had finally gotten this thing where I wanted it to be. My kids were in a great private school. Our church was thriving. I honestly didn't have a big desire to do this whole church-planting thing again. The first time nearly killed me. I was 40 years old now—let the younger guys do that! But deep down, I knew. When God said, "It's time to expand," He was talking about me.

For a long time, we had sensed God wanted us to expand, but we weren't sure how. I thought that after working so hard to develop and grow the church, that stirring for something more would go away. But it only grew—especially in Ken. I could see that fire burning inside him, something that needed to be fed. He had to keep his hands to the plow, so to speak, to keep his passion alive.

As I wrestled with the idea and sought counsel from mentors, God sent me multiple prophetic confirmations through trusted pastors and friends. They would say things like, I see you in another city. Little did they know, God was telling me the same thing. So, we started the process.

I decided to go to Jacksonville first and pray over the city. Surely, that was it—I had talked about Jacksonville for years. But when I went, I didn't feel or hear anything. Then I said, Let's drive to Tampa and pray over Tampa. I went, but it felt just like Jacksonville—nothing. So, I thought, "Okay, let's visit Orlando."

I saved Orlando for last because, truthfully, I never wanted to live in Orlando. I don't even know why. Maybe it was because I had so many friends there, and I felt like the city already had enough churches. It just wasn't in my prayers or on my heart at all—until…

I visited Orlando just like I had Tampa and Jacksonville. I was sitting in a Starbucks, meditating and praying, when I overheard a woman talking about real estate.

She was switching between Spanish and English effortlessly. In that moment, I felt the presence of God so strongly. It was as if He was confirming right then and there, This is where I have called you. It's time to expand.

Just like the call to Gainesville, I knew this was God. By now, I had become more acquainted with His voice and the way He called me to new seasons and new adventures. Even though I had never wanted to be in Orlando, I suddenly felt an overwhelming excitement. Finally, I thought, I know what He is saying. Yes, Lord, I will do whatever You want.

I knew it was Orlando the whole time. I feel like I had known it for years. It was just one of those things I tucked away in my heart, waiting for the right time. I never wanted to overstep my husband's role as the spiritual leader of our family. I felt like I knew, but what if God was telling him something else? Who was I to influence him in another direction? So, I prayed with him as he went through the process. And when he finally said Orlando, I was able to confirm, Yes, babe, it's Orlando.

I think it's so important for both spouses to give each other space to hear from God individually—especially the wife to the husband. There are many things I sense spiritually before Ken, but I've learned that most of the time, it's not my place to shove it down his throat. Just because God showed me something doesn't mean I'm supposed to push him into it. Instead, it's my job to pray it into the earth. I had been praying for our move to Orlando for years—long before my husband even wanted to come here. God just trusted me with enough information to intercede for it until the time was right. I believe that is one of the beautiful responsibilities of a wife.

After 12 years of ministry, God asked us to move again. Thankfully, this time it wasn't states away, but just two hours south of Gainesville to the vacation capital of the world—Orlando, Florida. At first, I didn't fully understand why, but in hindsight, this move made perfect sense to fulfill the "expand your territory" mandate. Orlando is the most visited city in the nation, with over 52 million people coming in each year. It's a hub to the nations, with an international airport bringing people from all over the world. Prophetically speaking, I believe the Holy Spirit has chosen Orlando as a gateway for what He wants to do globally. It is a spiritual portal, positioned for impact.

I was excited about the move. By this time, I had learned that when God says go, you just go. He knows you better than you know yourself, and He knows what you need before you even realize you need it. Our children were getting older, and this was a great opportunity for them to witness and be part of following God's leading. My younger two loved it. They were still in elementary school. My oldest was on board, but since she was in middle school—the most awkward of all years—it was a bit harder for her at first. But just as we knew she would, she eventually found friends and excelled in school. We made sure to include the kids in the process. Our oldest was with us when we found our first home in Orlando. Once the house was under contract, we brought the kids in to pick out their bedrooms and imagine where all the furniture would go. It made the transition fun for them.

This move was different from the first one. We weren't rookies anymore. We were seasoned pastors who had studied church growth, navigated spiritual battles, and survived the fire, famine, and flood. I knew that statistically, 90% of people on a new church plant launch team fall away within the first three years. Why? Not always for bad reasons, but studies suggest that many people are drawn to something *new*. However, as the church grows and their direct access to the pastors diminishes, or as they feel less essential to the work, they begin looking for something else. Other times, the camaraderie built through the struggle of setup and breakdown shifts once a permanent facility is established, and people don't feel as *needed*.

One of the greatest obstacles to the walk of faith is failed expectations. People get married expecting one thing, only to discover marriage is not what they imagined. The marriage isn't necessarily bad, but their disappointment comes from unmet expectations. People take jobs thinking they'll love them, only to realize it wasn't what they thought. The job might still be a good job, but they leave because of failed expectations. The same happens in the church world. Early in ministry, I suffered a lot of disappointment because I had subconscious expectations that weren't realistic. I assumed that because we had sacrificed to move to Gainesville, God would supernaturally protect us from financial struggles and that everyone would love and support us. Failed expectations. I had never been a youth pastor or an assistant pastor before launching our church. I came straight from the business world. I was *shocked* to see how some people mishandled the things of God. I naively thought every Christian would do a *180* like Tabatha and I had, leaving their past behind and fully committing to God. Again—failed expectations.

Coming to Orlando was different. I had learned. I set the bar low. I knew it would be a grind. We downsized our house. We lived beneath our means. We did everything we should have. We brought a couple of staff members with us to help with the load, but we still had to build a launch team from scratch—100+ people. I thought for sure more people from Gainesville would join us. But they didn't. Some of them came later, after the church was already built. We had to do this like any other church planter, despite only being two hours from our main campus. We quickly learned that Gainesville and Orlando are *very* different cities with very different needs.

I also assumed that everyone in Gainesville would fully understand our move to Orlando. After all, I wasn't leaving the church—I was expanding the church. But not everyone saw it that way. Some felt abandoned. In hindsight, part of that was my fault. Early in ministry, I had preached very strongly about staying plugged in and rooting yourself where God plants you. I meant that for those who were being pulled away for the wrong reasons, not to keep people from following God's call. I also never imagined I would be the one moving! But when the time came, I wasn't leaving the church; I was expanding it. Still, some viewed it as abandonment rather than expansion.

Abandonment issues are real. Many people have been abandoned by parents, spouses, or even past church leaders. Those wounds run deep, and it's easy to confuse new transitions with old trauma. It takes a mature believer to say, I'm not here for my pastor—I'm here because God called me here. Now let's go win some souls. Thankfully, we have so many people in Gainesville who have that mindset. They are the true heroes of this story. Their willingness to sacrifice their lead pastors, remain faithful to the vision, and continue giving generously is what has enabled us to expand our territory. I believe there's a special reward in heaven for them—and I pray they experience heaven on earth for their faithfulness.

But no church plant is easy. It doesn't matter how seasoned you are. You're still dealing with imperfect people, deadlines, budgets, and obstacles. By the time we planted Orlando, we had three kids. One was in eighth grade, one in fourth, and one in second. Only heaven knows how this move affected them. We moved about a year before launching, so we could build teams and prepare. The first five months of the church, we met in a high school—no facilities for teenagers, no dedicated prayer space, and limited programming. Then, five months in, COVID hit. For six months, we were buildingless.

When we resumed, we were renting space from another church with service times at 2:00 pm and 4:00 pm—not ideal for families. Kids' church was minimal, youth ministry was nonexistent, and that's how it was for two-and-a-half years. Only heaven knew the impact this had on our children and others who moved with us. No youth pastors, no dedicated youth ministry, no special events—just the grind of church planting. By the time I looked up, my eighth grader was in the middle of her sophomore year, and I thought, "How has all of this affected her faith?"

Nevertheless, I refuse to live in fear. When you say yes to the call of God, your treasure is always in the field. It might cost you something—there is always a price to be paid. However, we believe that God will work all things together for our good. A strong youth program can never replace the impact of a mother and father who boldly obey God, no matter the cost.

We are willing to trust God and let the chips fall where they may. That's one of the things I love most about my wife. There has never been a time when I said, "God said this," and she stood in the way. She has always been willing to forsake everything and follow God—or the God in me.

Believing Big

In the middle of the 2020 pandemic, the Lord gave us a word for the year: "Believing Big." At a time when fear paralyzed the world, when churches were closing, and we didn't know if we would ever meet in person again, God challenged us to believe beyond what we could see. What began as a short-term shutdown in March and April stretched into a way of life—masks, vaccine debates, social distancing. Yet, despite all of it, we had a word from the Lord: believe big.

Our school, where we had been meeting, shut down like all government-run facilities. We were forced to transition to online church, but in my heart, I knew that wasn't sustainable. We are a spiritual hospital. We needed to do whatever it took to reopen and minister to people in their deepest season of fear and uncertainty.

I expected some adversity while building the church, but I did not expect a global pandemic. How did we end up starting our church right at the onset of a pandemic? It was laughable! But I wasn't afraid. It was time for faith to rise up. I got out the anointing oil and prayed over my house and family. We encouraged everyone to trust in God. Like the rest of the world, we adapted—Zoom meetings, online services.

But perhaps the hardest thing about COVID wasn't the church transition—it was homeschooling. The kids and I tried our best, but it was rough. I had already attempted homeschooling once before and failed miserably. My kids wanted to tell me how to do the work instead of the other way around. They'd say, "But Mommy, why? But Mommy, why?" Inevitably, I'd resort to the classic, "Because I said so!" Then they'd cry, and I'd want to cry too. I put them back in school the next semester.

During COVID, they logged on while their teachers attempted to teach virtually. Poor teachers! I don't think my third and fifth graders learned anything new. But the comforting thing was that we weren't alone—the entire world was figuring it out as we went.

Thankfully, another local church allowed us to meet in their facilities after their morning services. But in my spirit, I knew God was about to provide a building of our own. Going back to a government-run school wasn't an option—I didn't want the government controlling when and where we could worship.

So, with my mask on, I went window shopping. I drove from building to building, looking through windows, dreaming. Then I came across an abandoned Office Depot building, right in front of the Florida Mall. It sat on a major road in the city, with a daily car count of 66,000 people. In Gainesville, our church was tucked away in a residential neighborhood. But now, when God said, "Expand," I couldn't imagine a better way to do it than getting into the middle of the city, where people could see us.

Along with a few board members, we toured several properties. Ken asked us to take notes and rank them. We gave our input, but really, we were just waiting to hear his thoughts. As a visionary, what was God showing him?

Then he told us he had a vision—an open heaven over the old Office Depot building. I threw up my hands. That's it! We all thought the same thing. Lead with that! There was no need to waste any more time. The one where God moved—that was the one!

So, we prayed, believed, and moved forward in faith.

There was only one problem—the building was way out of our price range. The owner was asking over $3 million just for the building, and it needed an additional $2 million in renovations. At the time, we didn't have anywhere close to that.

We kept looking. We needed somewhere to meet. We considered everything—rentals, purchases, event spaces. We had to bring back our Sunday morning services soon, or our little Orlando campus wouldn't make it out of the starting gates.

But for some reason, I couldn't stop thinking about that Office Depot building. It just felt right. One day in prayer, the Lord showed me a vision. It was like driving toward a rainstorm—you're in the sun, but up ahead, you see clouds and rain. Then He showed me that rainstorm inside the building. It was a vision of open heaven—a place where God would visit, where the sick would be healed, addictions broken, and marriages restored. I believed by faith that this building was ours. But then we got a call—the owner was considering an offer from Tesla.

It was like David and Goliath. Who was going to get the land? I reminded Ken, "If God has it for us, it's ours. No one can take it away."

For me, this was God vs. Tesla. And I knew God would win.

I fasted, prayed, and carried a picture of the building in my pocket. I drove past it constantly, laid hands on it, and prayed.

Then one day, we got a call—Tesla backed out. The owner wanted to talk. We initially planned to lease, but after presenting our terms, they went silent. Weeks passed. Then, the Lord spoke to me: "They don't want to lease. They want to sell."

With my real estate background, I started strategizing. What if they held the note? I proposed a deal:

$3 million purchase price

Seller holds the note for three years

5% interest rate

We fundraise aggressively and refinance within three years

The benefits for them? No more taxes, no more security costs, and they'd act as the bank, collecting monthly payments. If we succeeded, they'd get their money. If we failed, they'd reclaim the building. They agreed! We only put $150,000 down, and just like that—we were in the game!

Ken is a master negotiator. Negotiating makes me nervous, but he thrives in it. Back in D.C., we'd shop in Georgetown, where everything was negotiable. I hated it. I just wanted to see a price, pay it, and move on. But not Ken. Oh no, those poor salespeople had no idea who they were dealing with. He'd walk away with a whole wardrobe for pennies.

So, when it came to this contract, I knew—Ken would find a way.

We also negotiated six months of no mortgage payments. Our little campus couldn't handle a $20,000 monthly payment right away, so we needed time to grow. Then, a miracle happened. By the end of 2020, banks started lending again. Interest rates dropped, and somehow, we saved and fundraised $1.7 million. That changed everything. A bank stepped in, refinanced the entire $3 million, funded the $2 million renovations, and we paid off the seller in six months.

We never made a single monthly payment.

It was a miracle.

The Best of Times, The Worst of Times

We closed on our new property on December 4, 2020. It was the best of times. But at the same time, it was also the worst of times. I've always been amazed at how peaks and valleys in life can be so closely intertwined.

Tabatha wasn't at the settlement table that day because a few weeks prior, she had found a lump in her breast. Our settlement date just so happened to be the same day she was going in to get the results of her biopsy. But we weren't worried. We were sure it was just a cyst, nothing serious. She was so healthy, so in tune with her body, always mindful of everything she ate. So with all the faith in the world, she said, "You go to settlement for us, and I'll go to the doctor by myself… everything will be fine, and I'll call you after."

She went her way, and I went mine. But on the way home from settlement, I got a call.

"They say I have breast cancer."

Radio silence. I couldn't believe my ears. Was this April 1st? Was I being punked? Was I on Candid Camera? Please tell me this is a dream, and I'm about to wake up.

2020 was a roller coaster ride. We finally launched the church—woohoo! Then COVID hit—oh nooo! We found a church building—woohoo! Ken's mom was diagnosed with cancer—oh nooo! We settled on the property—woohoo! And then the big drop—I had cancer—ahhhhh!

As a man of faith, I believe that healing belongs to us. Jesus didn't just die for our sins; He died for our sicknesses too. I believe with all my heart that by His stripes, we were healed. Our healing was purchased with the broken body of Jesus and His resurrection over death. So I just didn't understand. How could God see our faith, see all the things we've given up for Him, and allow my sweet wife to go through breast cancer? Surely, God is going to heal her up front, and He'll get the glory…

I went to the doctor just to get a lump checked out. When she examined me, she found two lumps and ordered an ultrasound to get a better look. No biggie. Just doing our due diligence. During the ultrasound, they found a third lump and saw that my lymph nodes looked suspicious. In no uncertain terms, they told me I had cancer. The next step was seeing a breast surgeon for a biopsy.

When the results came back, I put the phone on speaker as the doctor gave us the news. "It's stage three breast cancer," she said, then went on to recommend a double mastectomy, chemotherapy, and radiation. Ken and I just sat there staring at each other in disbelief. For the first time, I looked at my husband, wanting to make everything okay, but I couldn't. I didn't have a pep talk. I didn't have a word. I had nothing.

I thought I knew a lot about the Kingdom of God and a lot about faith by this point. But pain has a way of teaching you things that promises never could. I always avoided the classroom of pain. I actually used to turn off preachers that talked too much about suffering, trials, and tribulations. I knew they were in the Bible, but we didn't need to talk about them. I'm a person of faith. I walk by faith and not by sight.

But I had to learn that just because you have faith doesn't mean you won't face attack, challenges, or an evil day. It's crazy how one moment can go from the best day to the worst day in a matter of seconds.

Honestly, after I got over the shock of it all, I got angry. Not at God—at the devil. The enemy comes to steal, kill, and destroy, but Jesus said, "I have come to give you life." I knew God had nothing to do with me getting cancer, but He would have everything to do with my deliverance from it. I thought, Devil, you tried it. How dare you put your hands on me? I was not playing around. Now more than ever, I had to believe that God would take what was meant for evil, turn it around, and make it work for my good.

The diagnosis was stage 3 breast cancer. My tumors had been there for a while. The plan was to go through five months of chemotherapy, three rounds of radiation, and a double mastectomy.

In my heart, I knew I should follow the lead of my doctors. But in my head, I had so many theories on natural medicine and alternative health treatments. I wanted to do all the natural things I'd been doing my whole life. But this cancer I was up against was trying to kill me, and I needed to use every weapon I could to kill it first. I was going to have to believe God if I didn't do what my doctors recommended, and I was going to have to believe God if I did. Either way, I had to have faith in God.

Tabatha was relentless. She cared more about her life than her hair. She cared more about her life than her breasts. She wanted to remove anything and everything that could cause cancer to come back. That was a hard pill to swallow.

We believed in functional medicine. We always have, and we always will lean more toward homeopathic treatments. We believe that with the right foods and environment, the body is designed to heal itself and protect against sickness altogether. If you have the right vitamins and avoid certain toxins, your immune system should be able to kill off cancer cells and any other germs or viruses that try to take over.

The hardest pill to swallow for us was, Why didn't our knowledge of functional medicine prevent this?

I did care about my hair. I loved my hair, and I cried when I finally realized I would lose it all. Then I felt vain for being concerned about my hair when my life was at stake. That's the ugly thing about breast cancer—it affects everything that makes you a woman. I was about to lose it all. My breasts, my hair, my eyelashes, my eyebrows, my fingernails, my periods—everything. Even my womb and ovaries through hysterectomy. It was a lot to accept. I just had to take it one step at a time.

The next step was telling our kids. We wanted to tell them in a way that wouldn't be scary but would help them have faith in God. We wanted them to take this journey with us and have a testimony of their own.

Our kids were 15, 11, and 9 at the time. They were old enough to understand that something serious was happening, but they weren't that deep. We stuck to the facts. We told them, "Mommy has to have surgery to take out the cancer, and then chemotherapy will be like medicine that will make my hair fall out. But after it's all done, the cancer will be gone, my hair will grow back, and we will have a celebration!"

We kept it positive and full of faith.

Modern medicine and functional medicine don't always see eye to eye. Modern medicine wants to burn it out and cut it out—chemo and surgery. Functional medicine wants to give you supplements and natural remedies to strengthen your immune system so it can destroy cancer cells without the harmful side effects of chemo and radiation.

We had a choice to make. Since we were talking *about her life,* we weren't about to take any chances.

So, we went with modern medicine. Get rid of this stuff!

I went into the fight full of faith. I believed that God would escort me to victory. We had so many kind people volunteering to bring food to the house and sit with me when

Ken couldn't be there. I did well after the double mastectomy. All of the breast tissue was removed, along with every trace of cancer. The doctors placed breast expanders so I could have reconstruction surgery after my treatments were over.

I also had drains extending from my chest that needed to be changed periodically. Ken was my nurse. He's really not good at those kinds of things, but he was right there every time I opened my eyes. The night after surgery, I needed to use the restroom so badly, but every time I stood up, I fainted and hit the floor. I remember coming back to and seeing Ken on the phone with my doctor. She said it was just the anesthesia and that I was okay. But that didn't change the fact that I still couldn't get off the floor or even stand up to go to the bathroom.

Once Ken knew I wasn't in danger, he did something genius. He propped me up against the bed, ran to his office, grabbed his desk chair with wheels, and rolled it over to me. Then he picked me up, sat me in the chair, and pushed me to the toilet where I could scoot myself onto it. See? Genius! For the next couple of days, that chair was my mode of transportation.

Next up was chemotherapy. The first month went well. I lost my hair but found out I didn't look like an alien underneath it all—that was a real concern! I decided to cut my hair early and donate it to an organization that makes wigs for kids fighting cancer. It gave me a sense of control in the middle of so much forced change. Ken sectioned my hair into ponytails and cut them off. Then he grabbed the clippers and shaved my head bald. What a day. I'd much rather take it off up front than watch it fall out little by little. From what I heard, that wasn't fun.

I have never met a stronger person than my wife. When I look over her past, I can see how God had been building her to handle hard things. But this was hard because I couldn't do anything to help her. Yes, we prayed. We had some of the most anointed healing evangelists of our day pray over her. We took communion daily. We stayed away from sugar. We did everything we could.

We are people of faith. And what we learned is that sometimes God delivers you from the fire, and sometimes He delivers you through it. For whatever reason, God decided to deliver us through this one.

Cutting her hair was hard. But we discovered that she has beautiful facial structure—those high cheekbones and features that looked just as stunning with or without hair.

The double mastectomy was hard too. As a husband, that was one of my favorite aspects of my wife. And the Bible backs me up on this one: "Let her breasts satisfy you at all times" (Proverbs 5:19). This wasn't just an attack on her—it was an attack on me too.

And then came the chemo treatments. Week after week, I had to watch her go through pain and despair, and there was nothing I could do about it.

About a month into chemo, something happened. I don't know if it was the change in drugs, my body growing weak, or a spiritual attack on my mind. Probably all three. But whatever it was, it broke me.

One night, I was sitting on the bed as we were getting ready to watch TV. Ken was settling down for the night, and the kids were still swirling around the room. I suddenly felt an unusual presence next to me. I turned to my left, expecting to see someone standing there. But nothing was there.

Immediately, I felt afraid.

Then I heard a voice—an evil voice that whispered: "You're going to die. Someone else is going to take your place."

I was surrounded by my whole family, yet they were clueless. Even I didn't fully grasp what had just begun. I immediately rebuked the thought and the demonic force behind it. Then I brushed it off and watched the movie with my family.

But later that night, I tossed and turned. That voice kept echoing in my mind. I began to see my husband and children moving on with their lives without me. I imagined myself missing out on their big moments—graduations, marriages, grandkids. I wanted to be there. I wanted to see my grandchildren. The thoughts wouldn't stop.

I prayed. I read my Bible. I quoted scripture. Ken had already put Post-it notes with affirmations all around the house—God loves me. I am healed. I am victorious. They were on every mirror, on doors, everywhere. But no matter what I did, the negativity wouldn't go away.

I didn't recognize myself anymore—inside or out.

I had many sleepless nights. Sleeping pills wouldn't even knock me out. I felt like I was going insane. One day, when Ken was gone, I either hallucinated or entered the worst spiritual battle of my life. I sensed overwhelming fear, and then I heard it—a high-pitched symphony of screams and cries. It sounded like hell.

After that, I never wanted to be alone again. But I kept fighting. I worshipped. I spoke the Word. But I was exhausted—physically, emotionally, spiritually exhausted. No hair, no eyebrows, no eyelashes. My body had grown thin and frail. My face was pale. My fingernails turned black and started falling off. I was always freezing. I felt like I was disappearing.

And I hated watching Ken watch me go through this. He was already taking care of the kids, the house, me, the church—everything. I didn't want to add to his plate. So, I found a counselor. And she helped me understand that yes, the thoughts were an attack from the enemy, but my response to them wasn't right. I rebuked the devil—which was good—but I never dealt with my own inner thoughts and emotions.

Our thoughts come from one of three places—God, the Devil, or ourselves. And sometimes, not every bad thought is from the devil. Sometimes, it's us. I had to stop rebuking my own feelings and start embracing them. Not accepting them, but acknowledging them.

"I feel afraid, and that's okay."

"Tabatha, why do you feel afraid?"

I started asking myself these questions—and answering them. People say that's crazy, but it's not. It's called being in touch with yourself.

And I found that these fears weren't just about cancer. They were tied to things all the way back from my childhood. And once I started addressing those things, one by one, the fear started to disappear.

God Speaks

I was journaling one day, feeling distant from God. I was still in the middle of my fight and couldn't see the light at the end of the tunnel. I wrote in my journal: "God, how can I trust You to heal me from cancer?"

And He answered with a question: "Do you trust Ken?"

I wrote back: "Yes."

He asked again: "Do you trust Ken?"

"Yes."

A third time: "Do you trust Ken?"

"Yes, I do."

Then He said: "If Ken had the cure for cancer, would he heal you?"

"Absolutely, he would."

And then God spoke His final question, which was more of a statement.

"How much more will I do for you?"

Like water in the desert.

I knew that I would make it through.

I knew that I could trust God.

In the middle of chemotherapy, something happened to me. I usually left the house early in the morning for a prayer walk around our neighborhood lake. There was a little dock with a bench where I'd sit, pray, and spend time with God. One day, as I was walking back from that spot, I had an encounter with His presence. It wasn't like the powerful encounter I had after 9/11, but it was just as real.

I felt the presence of God come over me, and I can only describe it as joy being injected into my veins. Suddenly, I felt light. I felt peace. I felt hope. In an instant, I knew I was going to make it through this. Long gone were the days of sadness and despair. Now, even in the middle of the storm, God was teaching me about joy.

I remember the day Ken came home from his walk. It was still dark outside when he left, like always. I got up to see Hannah off to the high school bus. Then Charity left for middle school. Kenny rode his bike to the elementary school around the corner. Once the kids were off, I went for my own morning walk—staying active made me feel alive.

When I got home, Ken walked in the door, eyes lit up, talking about this big revelation of joy. He said, "From now on, I'm enjoying everything! Life is good!"

Ken's eyes do this crazy thing when he gets excited—it's like fire lights up inside of them. I was just standing in the kitchen, thinking, Is he okay? Does he even know what I'm going through? I had so much discomfort in my body that I could barely see past the pain. But in my spirit, I knew he was right. I wanted what he had.

Later that day, I sat down and had him explain everything to me. He taught me what God had taught him. And in that moment, we both made a decision—we weren't just going to get through this, we were going to enjoy life in the middle of it.

So, we turned all the way up for joy. We started telling jokes, dancing, and watching funny movies. Charity would come home from school, and we'd binge The Cosby Show. We couldn't get enough of it. I even started dancing when I was alone. I'd do the running man so hard by myself that my stomach would hurt from laughing so much. (Seriously, you should try it!)

One of the funniest moments happened near the end of chemo. Ken and I would show up at the hospital, him in charge of carrying my ice cooler. One of the side effects of chemo was neuropathy—nerve damage in my hands and feet. So during every treatment, I wrapped my hands and feet in ice to prevent it. It worked, but it was so cold.

One day, my face started going numb too. So I went on Amazon and bought an ice-filled mask that covered my entire face. It had cut-outs for my eyes, nose, and mouth. I didn't think anything of it. I put the mask on, sat back in the treatment chair, and tried to acclimate. When I finally adjusted my eyes to see through the tiny holes, I caught a glimpse of Ken. He was staring at me like I had lost my mind.

"What is that?" he asked, dead serious.

I guess I forgot to tell him about the mask. I explained, and he handed me his phone. When I looked at the screen, I lost it. I looked insane. It was pitiful and hilarious at the same time. I busted out laughing, which gave Ken permission to bend over laughing too. It went on for way too long. We joked that when the nurse walked in, she was going to be terrified. We said I looked like the Abominable Snowman. It was so sad but so funny.

Looking back, I know we were passing the joy test.

We were learning to have joy, even in the hardest times.

At that time, I was taking care of our three kids, leading our church through a multi-million-dollar building project, and caring for my wife with stage three cancer. This kind of pressure could break a man. I could have easily fallen back into the depression of the earlier years in ministry. But God had done something in me. Not only had He matured my soul, but He had also given me an anointing for joy.

The Bible calls it the oil of joy.

Oil, in the Bible, often symbolizes the presence and power of the Holy Spirit. So, when the Bible talks about the oil of joy, I believe it's referring to supernatural joy—the kind of joy that sustains you even in the worst of times.

And remember—the joy of the Lord is our strength.

It was joy that carried me through.

It was joy that gave me a light heart again.

That day, God removed the reproach of the past, graced me for the present, and gave me a joyful perspective for the rest of my life.

This wasn't just some temporary encounter with God that lasted a few weeks or months. Years later, I'm still living in this joy. I have made it my daily mission to enjoy every second and to live with delight—and to teach others how to do the same. I learned that joy isn't just an emotion. It's a weapon. Joy is warfare. And the joy of the Lord is our strength.

On June 24, 2021, Tabatha received the call from the doctor's office. All her tests came back—she was cancer-free. Amazingly, the building was being finished at the same time her radiation treatments were wrapping up. Ironic, I know. I might not fully understand this connection until I get to heaven, but I will say this: What doesn't kill you will make you stronger.

One of the greatest things I learned through the cancer fight is that just because something bad happens to you doesn't mean you did something wrong. I tend to be a bit of a perfectionist. I like to follow the rules. I like to do the right thing. So when I got diagnosed with cancer, it felt like I had done something wrong, like I was being punished. I wracked my brain with questions—Did I not eat well enough? Did I not exercise enough? Am I a terrible person? What did I do to cause this? I guess deep down, I thought if I did everything right, then nothing wrong would come to me.

I now understand what the Bible says—In this world, you will have trouble. But take heart! I have overcome the world. Just because you're a believer doesn't mean everything will always go perfectly. But you will overcome.

Daniel was thrown into the lion's den, not because he was doing something wrong, but because he was doing everything right. He refused to pray to anyone except his God, the one true God. And yet, God didn't keep him from being thrown into the den—He was with him in it. God shut the mouths of the lions, and Daniel came out unharmed. I wanted God to deliver me from cancer, but instead, He walked me through it. If God doesn't deliver you from something, He will deliver you through it.

As of this writing, Tabatha has been cancer-free for four years. To God be the glory. Looking back over our lives, I'm still not sure why we had to go through everything we've been through. But we've learned to always *grow* through what we *go* through. I can honestly say I'm a better leader, a better husband, and a better Christian on this side of the battle than I was before it. That's not to say I'm inviting future battles—I'd love a season of peace, praise God. But no matter what you face, you always have two choices: Get bitter or get better. The choice is yours. We've chosen to use everything we've been through to draw closer to God and help others.

It was in the middle of the cancer journey that our current vision was birthed. I had a choice, like we all do—to get mad at God or to get mad at the devil. Too many people get mad at the wrong one. Satan is the author of confusion, sickness, and despair—not God. God is the One who wants to help, heal, and rescue us. If you get mad at God, you've believed the lie that He's to blame for what the devil is doing.

I had my own fork in the road. In the middle of my wife's battle, I decided that instead of getting angry at God, I was going to hurt the devil bad for the rest of my life. I asked myself, what can I do to make him pay for this? The answer was simple—win souls into the Kingdom for Jesus. In that moment, a clear direction for our future was born. Our church would dedicate itself to leading two million people to Jesus over the next twenty years.

People ask how our church is growing so fast. Honestly, I think it's because we let our pain push us into greater purpose.

Ken and I have always had a heart for marriages. It's part of our DNA, our story, and our calling. But we also knew we had to wait for the right season to step fully into that calling. Early in ministry, we would get vision from God and just go. But we've learned that just because God gives you a vision doesn't mean you're supposed to act on it right now. Timing is key.

People have been asking us for years, What are y'all doing for marriages? Are you going to do a marriage conference? A marriage podcast? We need help!

Over the years, we've been able to help so many couples overcome some of their toughest challenges. I think it's because we've always been real and willing to dig deep into our own relationship. That honesty helps us relate to people, and it helps them know they're not alone. I heard the people, I really did. But I also believed that the timing of people and the timing of God aren't always the same. So, we waited.

The idea to start a marriage podcast wasn't even that deep, honestly. I just asked myself, How can we best reach two million people in twenty years? How can we be authentically us while crossing denominational and religious lines? How can we reach people who don't even believe in God yet, but still add value to their lives and maybe introduce them to Jesus? The answer was simple—Let's do a marriage podcast!

We tossed around all these jazzy names for it, but at the end of the day, we realized that the best ministry we could give people was us. The Jesus-loving, raw, uncut, unfiltered us. Like it or lump it. Take it or leave it. This is us.

Our podcast is a tool we've given to God. We focus on helping married people and having real conversations for today's couples, but we also know that the principles we teach are valuable to anyone—single, married, divorced, or dating.

We firmly believe that when you get better, your marriage gets better. Marriage ministry isn't just talking about marriage all the time. You need family meetings. You need romance. You need to have sex with each other. You need to learn each other's love languages. But those are just tools.

Great marriages aren't built on tools. They're built on a change of heart. They're sustained by continual personal growth. That's why Doing Life with Ken & Tabatha isn't just a marriage podcast—it's a personal growth podcast with an emphasis on marriage.

We didn't start this podcast thinking about sponsorships or revenue. We just wanted to say, Here we are. Twenty-five years in. These are our battles, our bruises, and our blessings. Let's do life together. You are not alone.

And somehow, people seem to like it.

We thought about writing a book on marriage—sharing principles on communication, overcoming infidelity, breaking ungodly soul ties, and so on. But eventually, we said nah—let's just tell our love story. Let's let people see who we are and hopefully, they'll find God in our story.

Now, we have online marriage and pre-marriage courses, devotionals, and a vision for marriage conferences and events in the future. But at the end of the day, our mission remains simple: To help people grow closer to God and the people He's placed in their lives.

ten

TURNING IT AROUND

We've been married now for over 25 years. I joke all the time and say it's been the best 23 years of my life. And like with any good joke, there's always a little truth to it. The first two years of our marriage were rough. Really rough. But by the grace of God, we made it. We're here. We're best friends. And now, we get to help other couples turn their marriages around just like we did.

If your marriage is in a bad place, you're not alone. But if you keep doing the same old things, you're going to keep getting the same old results. If you want better, then better is possible. But you have to do some things differently to get different results.

Maybe your marriage isn't necessarily in trouble, but it's stale. It's on cruise control. You've lost the butterflies, and you want to get them back. Wherever you are, here are five key principles that helped us turn our marriage around. We pray they help you too.

1. Locate Where You Are

The law of destination starts with location. You can't get to where you want to go until you first identify where you are.

Our marriage was at its worst because I didn't even realize it was at its worst. That's dangerous. Ken knew things were bad—that's why he was wilding out. But me? I was oblivious. I was out of touch with reality, caught up in my own web of problems, caught in my own fog of depression. I couldn't see clearly. But the moment I got free from depression, I could see that our marriage was in trouble. The good news? Most troubles can be overcome—but you have to recognize them first. Once you see it, you can deal with it.

The first step to growth is knowing where you're starting from. So, ask yourself: Where is your marriage right now on a scale from one to ten? And more importantly—where do you want it to be? Do you even know what a healthy marriage looks like? Have you and your spouse ever sat down and defined what being a good husband or a good wife means in your relationship—not in theory, but for your actual life, your actual context?

Once you get honest about where you are, you can start charting a path toward where you want to be. That's when you begin restoring honor to the institution of marriage. You put some respect back on it. You stop coasting, stop pretending, stop ignoring the signs—and you start fighting to stop the bleeding.

For some couples, that means cutting off flirtatious relationships or walking away from emotional or physical affairs. For others, it means addressing things like addiction, abuse, pornography, dishonesty, or unchecked resentment. Whatever it is—if it's destroying your marriage, it has to go.

2. Work on Your Own Personal Growth

A marriage is the sum total of two people coming together. If one person is immature, selfish, or doesn't know how to handle conflict, it's going to affect the entire relationship. Now, we're not saying stop working on your marriage to work on yourself. You have to do both at the same time. But here's the truth:

Better me equals better marriage.

If you get better, your marriage will get better.

It's true—our marriage got better when I got better. I had a lot of junk in the trunk. So much baggage! In a perfect world, we would've worked through all of that before we said, "I do." But we don't live in a perfect world, and sometimes we've got to do some deep cleaning in our own souls.

I didn't start out thinking, I want to be a better wife. I started out thinking, I want to be a better person. I wanted to fully give my life to Jesus and learn His ways. As a result, I became a better wife. I wanted to bring the best version of me into our marriage.

So, ask yourself: Are you emotionally and spiritually mature? Are you growing as a person? Are you praying? Believing? Listening to God?

Do the inner work. Take responsibility for your role. Don't just pray for your spouse to change—ask God to start with you. It takes humility to grow. But when you change, everything around you starts to change too.

3. Die to Self

One of the greatest threats to any marriage is selfishness—being overly focused on your own wants, needs, and preferences. And one of the greatest tools for turning a marriage around is its opposite: selflessness. When we start putting the other person first, everything begins to shift.

Most of us get married because we want to share our lives with someone we love. We don't want to do life alone. But over time—when stress piles up, when exhaustion sets in—we start getting on each other's nerves. And suddenly, the person we once wanted to share everything with becomes the person we just want space from.

But here's the reality: most fights in marriage happen because one or both people aren't getting their way. That's it. It's not always deep. It's just pride, preference, and the desire to be right. So, what's the antidote? Start preferring your spouse. Choose to bless them. Ask questions like, "Where do you want to go?" or "What would make you feel loved today?" It's not about losing yourself—it's about learning how to love someone else well.

We started having what we called Bless Me Contests—seeing who could outdo the other in love, in kindness, in sacrifice. That one small shift changed the energy in our home. And more than anything, we both started praying, God, change me before ever praying, God, change them. That's where real transformation begins—when both people are willing to die to self so the marriage can live.

4. Stop Looking for an Easy Out

There's nothing new under the sun. The enemy doesn't need new tactics—he just keeps recycling the same old lies. He'll whisper that you married the wrong person. That life would be easier if you were alone. That you'd be happier with someone else.

But it's all a lie.

Marriage is hard sometimes. That's not a sign something's wrong—it's a sign you're human. Instead of looking for an exit ramp every time things get tough, it's time to dig in. To fight. To be the hero in your home.

We've seen too many couples threaten divorce like it's just part of the conversation. But when you keep divorce on the table, you'll never fully invest in the solution. What if, instead of threatening to leave, you committed to fighting for healing?

Get counseling—personally and together. Two years. Three years. However long it takes. Surround yourself with couples who are ahead of you and still in love. Join a small group. Listen to 100 podcasts. Read 50 books. Make it your mission to become an expert in your own marriage.

Because if you don't believe your marriage can be restored, you've already lost the fight. No boxer steps into the ring without believing they can win. So, take your gloves off the shelf and get back in the ring. The fight is worth it.

5. Put God First

The best marriage advice we could ever give you is this: Love God more than you love your spouse. When you love God first, He will help you love your spouse the way they need to be loved.

I can only love you the way I love God.

I can only honor you the way I honor God.

I can only submit to you the way I submit to God.

God is the creator of marriage. He's the only One who can truly restore and sustain it. The most important relationship in your life isn't with your spouse—it's with your Savior. If you have never made Jesus the Lord of your life, it's as simple as believing and surrendering.

Believe that Jesus came to this earth, lived a sinless life, and died a sinner's death on the cross. He was crucified thousands of years ago to pay the penalty for our sin. He was the spotless, blameless Lamb of God. He gave His life so that we could have eternal life with Him. But the story didn't end there—on the third day, He rose with all power in His hands, defeating death, hell, and the grave. Now, the Holy Spirit draws mankind into a relationship with Jesus.

You don't have to be perfect to be saved. You don't have to read the Bible cover to cover or have all the answers before taking a step toward Him. Really, all you have to do is surrender. Surrender means waving the white flag. It means giving up life your way and choosing to follow Him His way.

The truth is, we've all sinned. And no amount of good works or kindness can make us right with God on our own. Only Jesus can do that. When you accept Him as your Lord and Savior, you are transformed from a sinner to a saint—not because of your goodness, but because of His sacrifice.

For years, Tabatha lived without a relationship with Jesus. She will tell you—life with Jesus is so much better than life without Him. If you're humble enough to admit that you've sinned, and you're ready to surrender, I'd love for you to pray this prayer with me.

Wherever you are, whoever you are, you can come to God just as you are.

Pray this from your heart:

Lord Jesus, forgive me of my sins. I believe that You died on the cross to pay the price for my sin. Today, I choose to believe in You, and I also choose to surrender my life to You. From this day forward, I am Yours, and You are mine. Be my Lord and my Savior. I receive Your forgiveness by faith. I receive salvation by faith. I am a child of God. I am saved. In Jesus' name, Amen.

If you prayed that prayer for the first time, you've got to let us know! We want to pray for you, celebrate with you, and hear your salvation story. Maybe you're already saved and didn't pray that prayer, but you've been living as what we call a Christian Atheist—you believe in God, but you've been living like He doesn't exist.

Listen, marriage was God's idea. So, trying to do marriage without Him is like trying to build a house with no blueprint. If you're ready to rededicate your life to Jesus and invite Him into every part of your life—including your marriage—pray this prayer:

Lord Jesus, forgive me for living how *I* want to live instead of how You have called me to live. I have been a prodigal, but today, I am coming back to You. I ask for Your forgiveness, and as an act of my will, I recommit my life to You. You are not just my Savior—I want You to be my Lord. Lord of my feelings, Lord of my mindset, Lord of my finances, Lord of my sexuality, and Lord of my marriage. Thank You for forgiving me. Thank You for giving me a new beginning and a fresh start. In Jesus' name, Amen.

Congratulations on your spiritual decisions and commitments! We are proud of you and we believe that God is too.

Back to Butterflies

Is it possible to capture the butterfly feeling again? We believe it is. Maybe not in the exact same way from a chemical or hormonal standpoint, but if you're asking whether it's possible to live with awe, gratitude, wonder, amazement, intimacy, and attraction toward your spouse—our answer is absolutely!

Tabatha and I have been married for over 25 years, and even now, when I focus on how amazing she is, I can still feel those butterflies. It's not like when we first fell in love—back then, it was intoxicating. If that feeling lasted 24/7, I wouldn't be able to get anything done! But even now, while writing this book, I can still feel it.

You can totally bring back the butterflies. Start dreaming about your spouse again. Remember why you got butterflies in the first place. When you first fell in love, you couldn't stop thinking about them, talking about them, or imagining a future together. You were shopping for rings and dreaming of saying "yes." You can do that again!

Over the years, I've done little things to keep the freshness in our marriage. Yes, we're real with each other, and yes, we know each other's imperfections, but I draw the line at certain things. I'm never going to be comfortable with morning breath. I'm never going to let him in the bathroom if I'm doing a number two. I'll even leave the room to pass gas—if I accidentally let one slip, Ken turns into the flatulence police and makes a huge deal about it (just saying!). I'm always doing little things to keep him interested—a little perfume here, some essential oils there, maybe a new outfit just to keep him on his toes. Those things not only keep him attracted to me, but they also keep me thinking about him.

As you've probably figured out from this book, we are faith people. We refuse to live life based only on what we see. We are called to walk by faith and not by sight. That's not to say we ignore our feelings—God gave us feelings to enjoy life—but we are not dominated by them.

Many people feel like they've fallen out of love. We say, "What do your feelings have to do with it?" Many people feel like they're failures. We ask, "But what does God's Word say?" There have been times over the last 25 years when I've felt unsure, frustrated, stressed, or even like I wasn't in love with Tabatha anymore. But I don't allow my feelings to define me—I allow God's Word to define how I should feel.

With that understanding, we know we can live in a continual state of Butterfly Love. That feeling isn't just reserved for the infatuation stage—it can be something we cultivate and enjoy for the rest of our lives. The other night, I decided to test this theory. I asked myself, how do I really feel about Tabatha? I held her, I smelled her, I thought good thoughts toward her—and I felt the flutter. "It's still there," I said. "It's still there."

That moment reminded me of something I recently learned about God's presence. I love listening to podcasts, especially from people I respect. One of my favorites is the Grow Leader Podcast by Chris Hodges. He did an episode with Prophet Jim Laffoon called Hearing from God.

Jim talked about something I'd never heard before—the importance of stilling yourself to sense God's presence. He spoke about how busyness of the soul is one of the greatest attacks we face, and that often, our devices (phones, social media, distractions) are more of a threat to our spiritual life than the devil himself.

He explained that he makes it a practice to stop throughout the day—on a plane, in a meeting, wherever—and wait until he feels the presence of God. Not rush into prayer. Not start talking. Just stop. Be still. Wait. And he always finds that God is there.

I've started doing this daily, and I encourage you to try it too. Just pause. Right now, as you're reading this. Take a deep breath. Sense the presence of God. He's right there with you.

And that's how Butterfly Love works too.

You have to stop. Still yourself. Feel your spouse. Think about their heart. Reflect on your experiences together. Fill your mind and heart with appreciation and love. Hold them closely. Touch them. Smell them. Connect with them—not just physically, but emotionally and spiritually. I dare you to try it. If you can develop this discipline, you will get the butterflies back.

The Bible says, "Whatever is lovely, whatever is pure, whatever is of a good report—think on these things" (Philippians 4:8). I believe that what you focus on will expand. If you focus on the bad things—the quirks, the annoyances, the imperfections—those things will grow until they're all you see. But if you focus on the good things, they will grow until they become so big that you hardly notice the bad.

Have you ever had a friend who was dating the wrong person? Everyone knew that guy was bad news—except her. You tried to warn her, but she didn't listen, and she ended up heartbroken. That's what focus can do. She was so fixated on how handsome he was, how nice his car was, how charming he seemed, that she couldn't see that he was Shady McShade. Focus can work for you or against you. Make sure you focus on the right things in your marriage.

If you want to bring back the butterflies, you've got to remove the things that drive them away. There are certain enemies in your relationship that can make that spark fade, and if left unchecked, they will push you and your spouse farther apart.

1. Resentment

Resentment is that feeling of bitterness or frustration that builds up over time. It can come from small, repeated offenses or a few big ones, but either way, it poisons intimacy. If you're holding onto resentment, it's hard to see your spouse the way you used to. Resentment is one of the greatest enemies of Butterfly Love.

Be quick to forgive. In the words of Jesus, "You hypocrite, how can you point out the splinter in your brother's eye but ignore the log in your own?" When you're aware of your own faults and shortcomings, it makes it much easier to let go of resentment toward your spouse.

2. Criticism

Of course, there's constructive criticism—the kind that builds up. But there's also the negative, nitpicky kind, which we'll call fault-finding. And that kind of criticism slowly destroys love. Instead of focusing on what's wrong, try becoming the CEO (Chief Encouragement Officer) in your marriage.

I can naturally be negative. I have the ability to always find the thing that's off—which is great for fixing problems but not so great for a marriage. If I'm not careful, I can become a fault-finder. Criticism is an enemy of Butterfly Love.

Love covers a multitude of sins. God isn't following us around all day pointing out every flaw. If anyone has the right to do that, it's Him—but He doesn't. He covers us with grace. If God does that for us, why can't we do that for each other?

3. Busyness

Busyness is simply having a lot to do. And let me tell you—I am the poster child for busyness. I love having a full schedule and staying productive. But if I'm not careful, I'll be so caught up in what needs to be done that my wife gets the leftovers.

In the infatuation stage of a relationship, your spouse is your #1 priority. You go out of your way to make time for them. It's easy to feel butterflies when they are the main focus of your life. But after marriage, it's natural to shift that focus—now there are kids to raise, bills to pay, and careers to build. Still, if you want to maintain Butterfly Love, your marriage must be a priority again.

When Martha was overwhelmed with everything she had to do, she got upset with her sister Mary for not helping. Instead of working, Mary was sitting at Jesus' feet, listening to Him teach. Martha took her complaint straight to Jesus, saying,

"Make her help me!" But Jesus responded, "Martha, you are bothered about many things, but only one thing is necessary. Your sister Mary has chosen the good portion, and it will not be taken from her."

Mary prioritized her relationship with Jesus over everything else. And in marriage, every day there are many things to be done—but only one thing is necessary. Next to Jesus, your spouse is the good portion, the most important relationship you have on this earth.

4. Lack of Gratitude

Lack of gratitude is just another way of saying, "taking your spouse for granted." It happens when you get so used to them that you stop noticing all the good things about them. In the beginning, all you could see were their strengths. The flaws were still there, but your awe of them was so strong that you barely noticed. Over time, if you aren't intentional, the opposite happens—you only see the flaws and forget the good.

If you want to get the butterflies back, you've got to become grateful again. Appreciate who they are and what they bring to the table. If you don't, someone else will. There's a saying: One man's trash is another man's treasure. That's because one person sees what another has stopped noticing. Gratitude will bring back Butterfly Love faster than almost anything else.

Every good and perfect gift comes from above. Your spouse is a gift. And when God gives you a gift, you should treasure it. Never get tired of it. Never take it for granted.

It's crazy how we sometimes treat the people we love worse than we treat strangers. The more we know someone, the more comfortable we get—and unfortunately, that can sometimes mean less honor instead of more. It should be the opposite! The more we know someone, the more we should honor and cherish them.

5. Lack of Deep, Meaningful Physical Touch

Let's go back to the first time I told Tabatha, "I love you." Do you remember where we were? We weren't just on High Street, we were holding each other. She was sitting on my lap, leaning back on my shoulder. I had my arms wrapped around her waist. We were holding onto each other like we never wanted to let go.

Too many people get married and stop doing the things they used to do. They stop cuddling. They stop holding hands. They stop kissing just because. Sure, they still touch when it's time to have sex—but their relationship has shifted from passionate romance to more of a platonic partnership. They've lost the fire somewhere along the way.

But here's the thing—you can get that back.

I dare you to grab your spouse. Press your face against theirs. Smell them. Touch them. Hold them. Love them. Cherish them.

Deep, meaningful touch is essential to Butterfly Love.

Final Thoughts

We're sure there are more enemies of Butterfly Love than the five we've talked about. But this book isn't about everything that can go wrong in your relationship-it's about how to bring the love back and knowing that better is possible.

This is the story of two imperfect people who fell head over heels for each other, almost lost it all, and found their way back-again and again. It's not a fairytale. It's not a highlight reel. It's real life. It's about second chances. It's about grace. And it's about two people learning to serve an extraordinary God.

Butterfly Love is always there, waiting for you to tap back into it. For some couples, it may take more effort than others-but if you're willing to put in the work, you can get it back.

Once you remove the enemies of Butterfly Love, don't forget to add the right ingredients back in-intentionality, appreciation, priority, intimacy, fond thoughts, thoughtfulness, vulnerability, and trust. Take some time. Make a list. Start working on them, one by one.

If you're not sure where to start, we've created practical tools to help you on your journey including the Better Marriage Bootcamp, a 90-day online experience designed to help turn bad marriages into good ones, good ones into great ones, and great ones into out-of-this-world marriages. Learn more about the Bootcamp and all the other resources we have on our website at kenandtabatha.com.

We also invite you to check out our podcast and other resources like:

The Five Things Every Man Needs to Know About a Woman

The Five Things You Must Know Before You Get Married

How to Have a Family Meeting

Sex God's Way

These are the kinds of conversations that continue the journey long after the last page is turned.

We're not perfect at any of this, we're just committed to growth. We're chasing after God's best and sharing what we've learned along the way. Some of our stories went left. Some went right. Some will make you laugh. Some will make you cry. But that's real love in real life.

So, what happens when the butterflies go away?

You go catch them again.

I love butterflies. I have a little potted garden where I grow herbs, veggies, and the kinds of flowers that attract butterflies. Every spring, I get the urge to plant. And every year, without fail, the butterflies show up. At first, I thought it was random. But then I realized—they were drawn to something specific. Now, I plant with intention. I know what draws them in.

And I think marriage is like that. Most of us love butterflies. But even more than that, we all long for butterfly love—that fluttery feeling, that deep joy, that spark. And with your spouse, you can get it back. You don't have to settle for stale. Just plant the right flowers, and the butterflies will come.

Butterfly Love isn't just a book title. It's not just the first stage of a relationship. It's a lifestyle. And after 25 years, I'm still impressed with this Ken Claytor guy. I still blush when he says the wild things he says. I still fall for his ridiculous jokes. I still quiver when he whispers in my ear. I'm still in that butterfly love with Ken Claytor.

Our goal? To be 90 years old and still swept away with each other. That might not be probable—but it's definitely possible. And we pray this book helps you believe it's possible for you too.

To all the Butterfly Lovers out there—

Fly on.

Let's keep growing—together.

You were made for more. And your marriage was built to last.

APPENDIX

WE'D LOVE TO HEAR FROM YOU

Whether you've been impacted by this book, have questions about our ministry, or simply want to say hello, we'd be honored to hear your story.

Marriage is a journey and no one should walk it alone. If this book stirred something in your heart, sparked a conversation in your home, or reminded you that love is worth fighting for, let us know. Your story matters, and we're praying for God to keep writing beautiful chapters in your life.

You can find us, follow us, and reach out at:
Web: www.kenandtabatha.com
YouTube: @DoingLifewithKenandTabatha
Instagram: @kenclaytor | @tabathaclaytor
Email: info@kenandtabatha.com

We believe the best is still ahead—for your love story, your family, and your future.

GETTING THE BUTTERFLIES BACK

PRAYER FOR HUSBAND

Lord,

Thank You for the gift of my wife. Thank You for every moment we've shared, both the good and the hard, that has shaped our story. I confess that somewhere along the way, I may have stopped seeing her the way You do. I've allowed the weight of responsibility, distraction, or distance to dull the wonder I once felt. But today, I'm asking You to renew it.

Help me to see her with fresh eyes—not just as my wife, but as the incredible woman You've created her to be. Let me notice her laugh again. Admire her strength again. Pursue her again. Bring back the awe. Restore the tenderness. Rekindle the joy.

Make me the kind of man who leads with love, speaks with gentleness, and serves with humility. Help me remember why I fell in love—and give me the courage to fall in love all over again.

In Jesus' name, Amen.

GETTING THE BUTTERFLIES BACK

PRAYER FOR WIFE

Father,

You see every part of my heart. You know the longings I carry and the questions I don't always say out loud. There was a time I felt butterflies just hearing his voice. And though life has layered over that feeling with stress, routine, or disappointment, I believe You can bring back the beauty.

Restore the joy, Lord. Help me to laugh again. To notice the little things. To honor him not just in action, but in affection. Teach me how to love with fresh wonder, to let go of what has weighed me down, and to dream again with him.

I trust You to renew our connection. Thank You that what You bring together, You also sustain. I believe our best days are still ahead.

In Jesus' name, Amen.

ABOUT THE AUTHORS

Ken & Tabatha Claytor are the founding and lead pastors of Alive Church, a vibrant, multi-generational, multi-ethnic ministry with campuses in Gainesville, Orlando, Tampa, and online.

They are also the co-founders of the Alive Leadership Institute (ALI), a discipleship and leadership training program designed to equip believers to know God deeply, lead effectively, and walk in their God-given purpose. In addition, they host the annual Alive Conference, an encounter conference that draws people from around the world to experience healing, revival, and renewal.

Together, they carry a global mandate not only to preach the gospel, but to live it out in a way that transforms lives, restores hope, and tears down racial and cultural barriers. What began with just six adults in Gainesville has become a movement of thousands experiencing the presence and power of Jesus every week.

Ken is a passionate communicator, author, and visionary leader with a calling to raise up disciples and ignite revival across generations. Tabatha is the founder of PIO Woman, a growing movement that equips women to pioneer their lives with boldness, faith, and identity in Christ.

College sweethearts turned ministry partners, they've been married for over 25 years and continue to believe in the God who restores, redeems, and brings beauty from ashes. They live in Orlando, Florida and have three incredible children, Hannah, Charity, and Kenny.

And, of course, they still believe in the butterflies.

www.ingramcontent.com/pod-product-compliance
Lightning Source LLC
Chambersburg PA
CBHW022015120526
44580CB00015B/108/J